T0150652

BRISTOL ROVERS
On This Day

BRISTOL ROVERS
On This Day

History, Facts & Figures
from Every Day of the Year

STEPHEN BYRNE

BRISTOL ROVERS
On This Day

History, Facts & Figures from Every Day of the Year

All statistics, facts and figures are correct as of 1st August 2009

© Stephen Byrne

Stephen Byrne has asserted his rights in accordance with the Copyright, Designs and Patents Act 1988 to be identified as the author of this work.

Published By:
Pitch Publishing (Brighton) Ltd
A2 Yeoman Gate
Yeoman Way
Durrington
BN13 3QZ

Email: info@pitchpublishing.co.uk
Web: www.pitchpublishing.co.uk

First published 2009

A catalogue record for this book is available from the British Library.

10-digit ISBN: 1-9054114-9-9
13-digit ISBN: 978-1-9054114-9-8

Printed and bound in India by Replika Press Pvt. Ltd.

FOREWORD BY SAMMY IGOE

For any professional footballer, having the opportunity to play at Wembley Stadium is a dream. The 2006-07 season with Rovers provided me with many of the best moments in my career.

We reached the Johnstone's Paint Trophy Final at Cardiff's Millennium Stadium and the play-off final at Wembley in successive months. Didier Drogba, Richard Walker and I became the only three players to score on both grounds in the same season. My goal at Cardiff proved in vain, as Doncaster Rovers won 3-2 after extra time to win the JPT Trophy.

However, the final seconds at Wembley will live long in my mind. Time was up as Shrewsbury took a left-wing corner and, understandably, their goalkeeper came up in the hope of heading home a last-gasp equaliser. When this was headed clear, I picked the ball up on the edge of my own penalty area and knew the route to goal was clear. There is no accurate way to describe the wave of emotions that rush over you when you score in that fantastic stadium. More than that, though, we knew then, and the enormous mass of supporters behind the goal also knew, that Rovers had escaped finally from League Two.

I have enjoyed a long career in professional football, having the opportunities you dream of as a youngster. Martin Gregory's Portsmouth took me on as a teenager and I had six years at Fratton Park, before playing for Reading, Luton Town, Swindon Town, Millwall, Rovers and Hereford United. Recently, I played my part in Bournemouth's escape from the jaws of Conference football in the spring of 2009. When I came on as a substitute for my Rovers debut, we were trailing 2-1 at Cheltenham with three minutes remaining, yet the team scored twice to record a 3-2 win. This sums up the spirit in the Rovers camp at that time and explains why I was so happy to be a part of the successful Bristol Rovers side of 2006-07.

Sammy Igoe

ACKNOWLEDGEMENTS

No historical book could be compiled without considerable help from many sources. Pitch Publishing has been supportive and efficient throughout and Commissioning Editor Dan Tester has smoothed every path to enable this book to appear. Mike Jay is the author of numerous books on Bristol Rovers and I have had the honour of co-writing two club histories with him; his support and help has proved invaluable, not least with producing obscure photographs.

Mervyn Baker is a fount of knowledge about Bristol football, whilst Jim Creasy and Mike Davage are the definitive researchers into the career details of national footballers. Keith Brookman and Alan Lacock have offered generous help with details of Rovers' history and club photographer Alan Marshall has allowed unhindered access to his wealth of pictures covering generations of Rovers players. David Woods, the Bristol City historian, has shared freely his thorough and extensive records on late-Victorian football around the Bristol area.

I am extremely grateful to each of these people. And of course, nothing in life is possible without a loving and caring family. My wife, Stitch, who has been dragged to the occasional Rovers game over more than 20 years, is a constant source of love and support. Our children, Tolly, Ophelia, Horatio and Hatty are growing up to understand that Bristol Rovers is the only football club worth following.

INTRODUCTION

The rich tapestry of history is a feature of every community in the world and Bristol Rovers Football Club is no exception. As a child, I scoured the bookshelves, looking for books that might shed some light on the snippets of information that make up a history; I found no book there.

Over the past quarter of a century, a plethora of football history books have enabled the interested reader to understand much more about the background to each club. Mike Jay and I published *Pirates in Profile: Bristol Rovers Players Who's Who, 1920-94* in 1994 and *Bristol Rovers: The Definitive History 1883-2003* to raise the public's awareness of the rich and dynamic history behind Rovers.

I trust that this book will continue to inspire and encourage those interested in football and in social history.

Over the last few years, the Bristol Rovers matchday programme, *The Pirate*, edited by Keith Brookman, has been the recipient of several well-deserved accolades. As the 2008-09 season drew to a close, it was voted best programme in its division by *Programme Monthly* for the sixth year in succession.

The historical angle in these publications has been heavily promoted and I am very grateful to have been given the opportunity to write so much for every single home match over 16 years. As I take my growing family overseas in August 2009, I will have to sever the link with the programme.

This appears an appropriate time for an *On This Day* book to appear on the bookshelves. I trust that what appears in this book will be of interest to the many supporters who have commented so generously down the years on the content of my articles.

Stephen Byrne, 2009

BRISTOL ROVERS
On This Day

JANUARY

SATURDAY 1st JANUARY 1921

Alf Tirrell became the first of only eight players to score for both sides in a league game involving Rovers. Before a 6,000 crowd at Kenilworth Road, Sid Leigh's early goal had given Rovers a first-half lead against Luton Town that Tirrell's well-taken free kick had cancelled out. As half-time approached, Tirrell deflected Leigh's shot off the greasy turf past his own goalkeeper to give Rovers a 2-1 win. Luton's Ernie Simms missed a late penalty, his spot kick being saved by Rovers' goalkeeper Jesse Whatley.

THURSDAY 1st JANUARY 1987

A crowd of 17,122, at an 11.30 am kick-off at Ashton Gate, was treated to a highly memorable local derby. Bristol City were flying high in the table and they swiftly put lowly Rovers to the sword. City had eleven shots on target to Rovers' two and, in addition, Paul Fitzpatrick and Steve Neville both hit Rovers' bar; Rovers also lost goalkeeper Tim Carter for 15 minutes through injury and midfielder David Mehew went in goal. Then, astonishingly, midfielder Gary Smart's long-range shot after 87 minutes dipped under the bar to give Rovers an implausible 1-0 victory.

SATURDAY 2nd JANUARY 1897

Rovers arrived 40 minutes late for an extraordinary Western League encounter at Bedminster. John McLean scored after 25 minutes and Bill Stone's goal put Rovers 2-0 ahead a minute before half-time. However, a second-half brawl saw Rovers reduced to nine men, with both Novello Shenton and Charlie Leese being sent off, along with Baugh of Bedminster. Then goalkeeper Louis Johns left the field injured and, though McAuliffe pulled a goal back, eight-man Rovers held on for an unlikely victory.

MONDAY 3rd JANUARY 2005

Brian Cash spent eleven minutes on the field as a Rovers player. He came on as a substitute in the 79th minute of the home game with Northampton Town, which Rovers won 3-1, and was himself substituted by Elliott Ward in stoppage time. His subsequent fall-out with manager Ian Atkins spelled the end of his time with Rovers. An Eire under-23 international, Cash also represented Nottingham Forest, Swansea City and Rochdale in the Football League.

SATURDAY 4TH JANUARY 1986

Two Trevor Morgan goals, and one from Byron Stevenson, earned Rovers a 3-1 FA Cup third round win at Eastville against top-flight Leicester City. Five minutes after half-time, Stevenson put Rovers ahead with a free kick and, with the 9,392 crowd still buzzing, Morgan swiftly added a second off the far post. Sixteen minutes from time Morgan added the third before Gary McAllister pulled a goal back from the penalty spot. It was Rovers' first FA Cup victory over top division opposition for 28 years.

SATURDAY 5TH JANUARY 1924

Crowd trouble is not a new phenomenon. When Rovers lost 4-3 at home to Bournemouth, there was a disturbance at half-time. As Rovers trailed 3-2, a drunken spectator attacked referee R. R. Crump and was ejected from the ground. Rovers received a warning, as there had also been an incident at a reserve game earlier in the season. In addition, there had been trouble at two reserve games in the spring of 1922, at home to their opposite numbers from Portsmouth and Luton Town.

SUNDAY 6TH JANUARY 1974

During the mid-1970s the three-day-week imposed because of national power cuts meant that floodlights could not be used. As a result, some games were played on Sundays and Rovers' first Sunday fixture was the FA Cup-tie against Nottingham Forest. Though Frankie Prince, Colin Dobson and John Rudge all scored, Rovers lost 4-3. The first Sunday Football League game came against Aldershot three weeks later, whilst the first home Sunday game was the 2-2 draw with Newport County in December 1986.

SUNDAY 6TH JANUARY 2002

Given Rovers' poor league status, this seventh FA Cup victory over top-flight opposition was arguably the most impressive. It was only the second time that Rovers had won a game in this competition on the ground of a top division side and the score belied Rovers' position three leagues lower. Nathan Ellington became the first Rovers player to score a hat-trick away from home in the FA Cup, scoring after 14, 40 and 62 minutes, before Fabrizio Ravanelli scrambled home a consolation goal for Derby County two minutes from time. The 6,602 away supporters in the 18,549 crowd constitutes a record at Pride Park that stands to this day.

SATURDAY 7TH JANUARY 1956

Matt Busby's Manchester United side came to Eastville for a third round clash in the FA Cup that was described in the *Bristol Evening Post* as 'Rovers' finest hour'. Although Duncan Edwards was injured, the reigning league champions attracted a crowd of 35,872 to Eastville and five of the United side sadly were to perish in the Munich air crash two years later. Alfie Biggs scored twice, and Barrie Meyer and Geoff Bradford once each, as Rovers recorded a 4-0 victory. They were, according to Desmond Hackett in the *Daily Express*, 'the £110 team with the million-dollar touch of class'.

SATURDAY 8TH JANUARY 1955

A new ground record of 35,921 at Eastville saw Rovers defeat top-flight Portsmouth in the FA Cup. Rovers' 2-1 victory came courtesy of Geoff Bradford and Bill Roost, who both scored past the Northern Ireland international goalkeeper Norman Uprichard. John Gordon replied for Pompey. The ground record was again broken, though, in the fourth round, when Rovers entertained the champions-elect Chelsea.

SATURDAY 9TH JANUARY 1932

Because of heavy fog, Rovers left their normal transport behind and dashed for Southend United's ground in a fleet of taxis, arriving just 15 minutes before kick-off. Although visibility was very poor, the Third Division (South) fixture went ahead anyway and Rovers, trailing 2-0 by half-time, managed just a consolation goal from Ronnie Dix in a 4-1 defeat before a crowd of 6,220. Jimmy Shankly, the brother of the future Liverpool manager Bill Shankly, scored twice for the Shrimpers.

TUESDAY 9TH JANUARY 1996

The first Golden Goal scored by Rovers was netted against Fulham at Craven Cottage by Marcus Stewart. It was Stewart's second goal of the game, as Rovers won an Auto Windscreens Shield Southern Section quarter-final 2-1 in extra time. Duncan Jupp scored for Fulham. Two years later, Walsall's Roger Boli knocked Rovers out of the same competition with an extra-time Golden Goal.

WEDNESDAY 10TH JANUARY 1951

Rovers' long FA Cup run, which took them to an unprecedented quarter-final place, continued apace, thanks to a dramatic start in front of a 10,000 crowd at Eastville. After just eight seconds – the second fastest goal in Rovers' history – Vic Lambden fired ahead against Aldershot and went on to complete a hat-trick as the Hampshire visitors were defeated 5-1 in this third round tie; Bill Roost and George Petherbridge also got on the score-sheet.

SATURDAY 10TH JANUARY 1976

The earliest that Rovers have used a substitute in a league game is the very first minute of a match. Gordon Fearnley picked up an injury in the opening seconds at Fulham and was replaced by Bruce Bannister. The substitute was to score the only goal of the game as Rovers recorded a win in front of a crowd of 7,863 at Eastville.

SATURDAY 11TH JANUARY 1913

Prior to World War One, the only occasion that Rovers defeated a First Division club was the 2-0 FA Cup victory over Notts County at Eastville before a 15,000 crowd. Despite eight hours of heavy rain, the game went ahead and Harry Roe's low shot after 25 minutes skidded home through the mud to put Rovers ahead. Seven minutes from time, Billy Peplow's cross was turned in by Jimmy Shervey, with the aid of a deflection off County's right-back Herbert Morley. One footnote to this giant-killing story is that, at six feet five-and-a-quarter inches, County's goalkeeper Albert Iremonger was the tallest opponent Rovers faced until the 1980s.

SATURDAY 11TH JANUARY 1936

Victory over Oldham Athletic brought Arsenal, arguably the biggest name at that time in world football, to Eastville for an FA Cup-tie. This game drew a crowd of 24,234, which produced takings of £3,552. Incredibly, after Jack Ellis had saved a penalty from Arsenal's Cliff Bastin, Rovers took the lead three minutes from half-time, as Harold 'Happy' Houghton shot home from the edge of the penalty area. After half-time, though, the floodgates opened and Arsenal won 5-1, with Bastin and Ted Drake scoring twice each and Edwin Bowden once. Arsenal beat Sheffield United in that year's FA Cup Final at Wembley.

SATURDAY 12TH JANUARY 1952

FA Cup victories over Kettering Town and Weymouth earned Rovers a plum third round tie at home to First Division Preston North End, who could boast players of the calibre of Tommy Docherty and Charlie Wayman in their line-up. The 30,681 spectators were not disappointed, either, as Rovers defeated their illustrious opponents 2-0 through Geoff Bradford's angled first-half drive and Vic Lambden's close-range effort 13 minutes from time. Preston finished that league season in seventh place.

SATURDAY 13TH JANUARY 1973

Dick Sheppard, playing in his 150th league match for Rovers, suffered a depressed fracture of the skull whilst playing in goal, in an accidental collision with Eddie Loyden of Tranmere Rovers. He was to appear just one more time in Rovers' colours. The 2-0 win was played before an Eastville crowd of 8,909 with winger Colin Dobson claiming both goals.

SATURDAY 14TH JANUARY 1888

Rovers' first-ever cup-tie was a Gloucestershire Cup match played at Bell Hill, away to a strong Clifton Association side, who wore 'chocolate and cardinal' shirts and defeated Rovers 4-1. Rovers lost Bob Horsey after only two minutes, with a strained leg muscle, and were forced to play the rest of the match a man short. Against the odds, outside-left Bill Bush gave Rovers the lead five minutes before half-time. Arthur Beadon Colthurst equalised moments before the break and scored again after 55 minutes. Charles Wreford-Brown, the first Bristolian to play for England, had put his side 2-1 up after 50 minutes and Harry Francis, who was to play cricket for South Africa in two Test matches a decade later, completed the scoring two minutes from time.

FRIDAY 15TH JANUARY 1886

Peter Roney was born in Glasgow. Formerly with Ayr United and Norwich City, he joined Rovers in May 1909 and played in 178 Southern League games becoming, in the process, the only Rovers goalkeeper to score a competitive goal, as he converted a penalty against Queens Park Rangers in April 1910. He served in the 17th Middlesex Regiment (Footballers' Battalion) in World War One, but was traumatised by the war and was seriously ill through the 1920s. He died in Clydebank in August 1930.

SATURDAY 16TH JANUARY 1909

Through more than a century of Rovers' history, the fastest hat-trick scored by an opponent in a competitive fixture was that scored by Burnley's Arthur Ogden in an FA Cup tie. Ogden struck after 60, 63 and 66 minutes to register three goals in six minutes. Second Division Burnley won the match 4-1, with Richard Smith scoring their other goal and Billy Peplow replying for Rovers before a crowd of 7,000 at Eastville. The fastest hat-trick scored by any Rovers player was that recorded by Dai Ward against Doncaster Rovers in December 1956, when he scored after 77, 78 and 80 minutes to register three strikes in four minutes; both Vic Lambden and Peter Beadle have registered nine-minute hat-tricks for Rovers in the league.

WEDNESDAY 16TH JANUARY 1935

There were only 1,500 hardy souls at Eastville for the visit of Northampton Town, the lowest home crowd in Rovers' Football League years, but they were rewarded for their perseverance with a comprehensive 7-1 win, the largest so far since Rovers had entered the Football League in 1920. Goalkeeper Jack Ellis was injured and Somerset cricketer Newman Bunce was given a debut in goal, but he was rarely troubled as Rovers ran in seven goals, with George McNestry and Albert Taylor scoring twice each. Dick Brown missed a penalty for Northampton. The visitors were to drop seven of their side, including goalscorer Tommy Bell, for their next game.

SATURDAY 16TH JANUARY 1999

One of the most remarkable scores in Rovers' history was the 6-0 win against Reading at the Berkshire side's new Madejski Stadium. Reading had won their previous game 4-0 but, after a goalless first-half, Rover scored six times without reply in the space of 41 second-half minutes. Jamie Cureton scored the first four goals, one a penalty, only the eleventh occasion that any Rovers player had scored so many in a league encounter, and Jason Roberts added two more in the final moments. Cureton, thus the first opponent to score a hat-trick at this new stadium, later became the first home player to do so when, having joined Reading, he scored three times against Brentford in September 2000.

SATURDAY 17th JANUARY 1931

Tom Crilly, the Crystal Palace defender, conceded an own goal as Bristol Rovers defeated their opponents 2-0 before a crowd of 14,849 at Selhurst Park, Ronnie Dix also scoring. What is noteworthy about this is that Crilly had previously also scored an own goal in favour of Bristol City, when his side Derby County had lost 3-2 to the Robins at the Baseball Ground in September 1923. Essentially, Tom Crilly had scored for both Bristol clubs in the league without ever playing for either!

SATURDAY 18th JANUARY 1997

Andy Tillson was booked after just 20 seconds – the fastest booking for any Bristol Rovers player – in conceding a penalty, through which Nigel Pepper gave York City the lead. After such a dramatic start, this league match could not maintain the level of excitement and was to finish 1-1 with Peter Beadle's equaliser all the 4,470 crowd had to cheer.

SATURDAY 19th JANUARY 1889

The first time Rovers are recorded as having scored a first-minute goal was when Fred Channing scored against Southville. This game, played at Three Acres, was to finish 1-0 in Rovers' favour and was refereed by W. G. Grace, the famous England cricketer, who was a local medical doctor and often refereed local football matches during this era. Dr Grace was a supporter of local football and ran a surgery from Stapleton Road, within a cricket ball's throw of Rovers' pitch at this time.

SATURDAY 19th JANUARY 1957

Having lost 7-2 at Bury just over three weeks earlier, Rovers proceeded to lose by the same score at Leicester City's Filbert Street in front of a crowd of 32,288. This is the only league game featuring Rovers when four separate players have scored twice each. Peter Hooper did so for Rovers, as did Tommy McDonald, Arthur Rowley and Billy Wright; Derek Hines scored once. Rowley – who had also scored in the fixture at Eastville earlier that season – remains, to this day, the record aggregate goalscorer in Football League history with 434 league goals to his name.

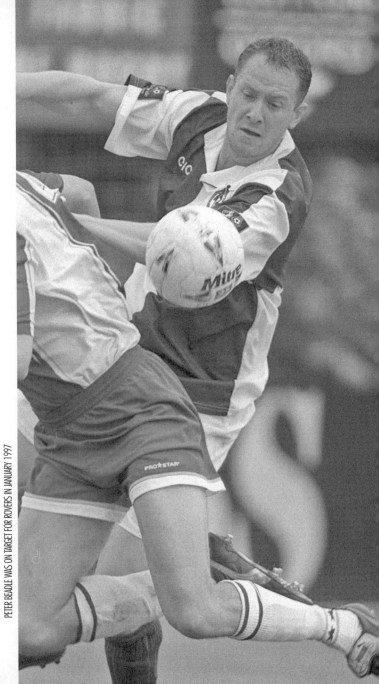

PETER BEADLE WAS ON TARGET FOR ROVERS IN JANUARY 1997

SUNDAY 20TH JANUARY 1895

Jesse Whatley, one of the most popular players in Rovers' long history, was born in Trowbridge. Over six feet tall, Whatley was the club's regular goalkeeper in the first decade in the Football League, playing in 14 Southern League games during the 1919-20 season, and 374 league matches between 1920 and his retirement in 1930. An England trialist in 1924 – a major achievement for a Third division player – Whatley followed Rovers' fortunes up to his death in March 1982.

SATURDAY 20TH JANUARY 1962

Although Rovers lost 2-0 before a crowd of 8,852 at the Victoria Ground, no Stoke City player's name was on the score-sheet. Six minutes before half-time, David Pyle deflected a harmless-looking cross from Don Ratcliffe into his own net and Norman Sykes, who had also conceded an own goal at Roker Park seven days earlier, turned in another Ratcliffe cross after 66 minutes. At half-time the referee R. H. Mann of Worcester – who took charge of that season's League Cup Final second leg – had to retire after pulling a leg muscle and was replaced by J. W. Tucker of Loughrane.

SATURDAY 21ST JANUARY 1933

Watford defeated Rovers 3-1 at Vicarage Road in a Third Division (South) fixture in front of a crowd of 4,202, with Tom Wyper scoring Rovers' goal, one of only two he registered in Rovers' colours. Arthur Woolliscroft, Jack Barnes and Mick O'Brien, from the penalty spot, all scored for Watford. In doing so, O'Brien became the oldest player ever to have scored a penalty against Rovers; he was 39 years 164 days.

SATURDAY 21ST JANUARY 1984

Rovers recorded a 2-1 victory away to Exeter City in Division Three thanks to a Simon Webster own goal and a rare strike from left-back Neil Slatter. Ray Pratt scored the home side's goal in a match watched by a crowd of 5,310. At the final whistle, some so-called Rovers 'supporters' charged across the pitch towards Exeter fans. Sixty police officers dealt with the trouble, six policemen were injured and 24 troublemakers were arrested.

TUESDAY 22ND JANUARY 2008

Tenacious and determined, and cheered on by a partisan crowd, Rovers were 'vastly superior in terms of both adventure and endeavour on a famous night' (James Corrigan, *The Independent*). Rovers had drawn 2-2 away to top-flight Fulham in the FA Cup having twice taken the lead through central defenders Danny Coles and Craig Hinton. In the replay, following a goalless draw, Rovers triumphed 5-3 on penalties, with Craig Disley, as he had against Leyton Orient in an earlier round, converting the decisive spot kick.

SUNDAY 23RD JANUARY 1955

Jock Bethune died in Sittingbourne, Kent, at the age of 66. A Scottish-born full-back, he had played for Heart of Midlothian and Barnsley before arriving at Eastville in May 1920. During Rovers' inaugural season in the Football League, he played in 30 league matches without scoring and later played for Brentford. Bethune, though a Scotsman, represented England at indoor bowls in the series of 1936 and 1938.

SATURDAY 24TH JANUARY 1903

The celebrated C B Fry was at right-back for Portsmouth as Rovers lost 3-0 on the south coast in the Southern League. Charles Burgess Fry played football for England, appeared for Southampton in the 1903 FA Cup final; represented England at cricket in 26 Tests; and held the world long-jump record. Later, he published his own magazine, stood for parliament, represented India at the League of Nations and famously declined the Kingship of Albania.

SATURDAY 24TH JANUARY 1925

Dense fog was the story of Rovers' home game with Northampton Town, which the visitors won 2-0. The fog was such that the identity of the first goalscorer is heavily disputed. The reporters on the touchline could not see either goalmouth, let alone identify whether Bill Poyntz or, as seems more likely, Ernie Cockle had given the visitors the lead. Quite what the 6,000 crowd made of it all remains a mystery.

SATURDAY 24TH JANUARY 1981

Despite a Geraint Williams goal, Rovers crashed out of the FA Cup 3-1 to Southampton, before a crowd of 23,597 at The Dell. Steve Moran scored once in each half for the Saints and midfielder Steve Williams also scored.

SATURDAY 25TH JANUARY 1936

Jack Woodman's second-half equaliser earned Rovers a point at Southend United in a 1-1 draw in Division Three (South), watched by a crowd of 6,005. The home side had led at the interval through a Leo Stevens goal. Prior to the game, there was a one-minute silence to remember King George V, who had died five days earlier.

SATURDAY 26TH JANUARY 1895

The first penalty Rovers were ever awarded came in a game against Mangotsfield and was successfully converted by club captain Hugh McBain. Despite the milestone spot kick, Rovers lost this Gloucestershire Cup-tie 5-3. Born in Inverness in 1869, the son of Andrew and Jessie McBain, Hugh McBain was brought up in the enigmatically-named Loch Street in Inverness and arrived at Rovers as captain in 1893. He played 97 times as a wing-half for the club, scoring twelve times, and also represented the Bristol and District XI against Aston Villa in 1894 at the opening of the Bell Hill Ground, a game that was lost 8-0.

SATURDAY 27TH JANUARY 1934

Rovers reserves beat Cheltenham Town 12-1, with Jimmy Smith scoring four times and George Tadman three. Edwards scored twice, with Doug Lewis, Billy Jackson and Gill scoring a goal apiece; Hazard scored for Cheltenham Town. Cheltenham's stock rose to the extent that they entered the Football League in 1999 and, by the 2001-02 season, were playing Rovers' first team competitively.

TUESDAY 28TH JANUARY 1958

Until 2007, the only time Rovers had won a fixture in front of a crowd exceeding 40,000 had been the astonishing 3-2 FA Cup victory away to First Division Burnley. Rovers could feel proud that they had held their strong opponents to a 2-2 draw at Eastville, but better was to come at Turf Moor. Norman Sykes scored his first goal for a year and Dai Ward added two more as Rovers notched a famous 3-2 victory. Prior to the victory at Derby County in January 2002, this was the only time Rovers had won an FA Cup tie on the ground of Division One opposition.

WEDNESDAY 29TH JANUARY 1902

Middlesbrough, a strong First Division side, were expected to defeat Southern League Rovers comfortably in the FA Cup but, after Rovers had drawn 1-1 at Ayresome Park, the minnows pulled off a controversial replay win at Eastville in front of a crowd of 7,586. Before the game could take place, Boro officials discovered that Rovers' goalposts were an inch shorter than the regulations stipulated; however, the Football Association rejected their protests. Three minutes from time, Bill Wardrope missed an excellent opportunity to win the game for the visitors, and Rovers broke for Tommy Becton to fire home for a famous victory.

SATURDAY 29TH JANUARY 1927

Conceding two penalties at the Goldstone Ground for a second consecutive season, Rovers lost a Third Division (South) fixture 7-0 against Brighton in front of a crowd of 7,472. On his sole league appearance, Jimmy Kedens broke clear in the first minute, but this was to be Rovers' only opportunity. Paul Mooney converted the second penalty, after Bill Little had missed the first. Future Rovers forward Tommy Cook was on the score-sheet.

SATURDAY 29TH JANUARY 1949

Having been knocked out of the FA Cup by Walsall, Rovers took advantage of a free weekend to invite the mighty Newcastle United to Eastville for a friendly. The visit of the top division side – three-time cup winners in the early 1950s – drew a crowd of 25,855 to Eastville. Rovers were holding their prestigious opponents 1-1 after 65 minutes, when the fog descended and the game sadly had to be abandoned. Two years later Rovers met the same opposition in two epic FA Cup quarter-final matches.

SATURDAY 30TH JANUARY 1960

The largest crowd at any Rovers home match down the years was the 38,472 that gathered at Eastville for an FA Cup-tie against Preston North End. The huge gathering was not disappointed, either, as the sides served up a six-goal thriller. Alfie Biggs scored twice for Rovers and Jim Smith conceded an own goal, whilst the legendary Tom Finney contributed one of the visitors' three goals. North End won the replay 5-1 at Deepdale.

SATURDAY 30TH JANUARY 1937

Having played in 92 league games for Rovers, scoring once, Sid Wallington rejoined Rovers from Guildford City in time to make two further league appearances. Born in Birmingham in October 1908, this slender wing-half had played for Birmingham City prior to his arrival at Eastville in August 1933 and was to move to Worcester City in May 1937. Wounded in action in the Second World War, Wallington died in Birmingham in December 1989, aged 81.

TUESDAY 31ST JANUARY 1956

The fact that Rovers lost an FA Cup-tie to a first-half goal from Bert Tindill at Doncaster Rovers pales into insignificance compared with the broken leg sustained in this game that kept Geoff Bradford out for the rest of the season. The talismanic Bradford, who had played for England earlier that season, had scored 25 league goals that campaign – and there were still 15 matches remaining. In his absence, Rovers narrowly missed out on promotion to the top flight and, having never yet attained such heights, Rovers can look back on Bradford's injury as a critical moment in the club's quest for success.

SATURDAY 31ST JANUARY 1987

Just a cluster of Rovers supporters at Field Mill, where the overall attendance was only 2,718, saw Rovers crash 5-0 to Mansfield Town in a Third Division fixture. Keith Cassells, a London-born striker, became only the eighth opponent to score four times against Rovers in a league encounter. Three goals ahead at the break, Mansfield won at a canter, with veteran striker Neil Whatmore also scoring past goalkeeper Tim Carter.

SATURDAY 31ST JANUARY 1998

Of all Rovers players sent off, the youngest was Luke Basford. He was less than three months past his 17th birthday when he received a red card during Rovers' 1-1 draw at Gillingham. Before a crowd of 5,593 at the Priestfield Stadium, Rovers fell behind to an Iffy Onuora goal after just 38 seconds and equalised seven minutes before half-time, when Jamie Cureton successfully converted a penalty.

BRISTOL ROVERS
On This Day

FEBRUARY

WEDNESDAY 1st FEBRUARY 1905

Joe Pointon, a Rovers forward in the 1930-31 season, was born in the Staffordshire town of Leek. Formerly with Port Vale, Luton Town, Brighton & Hove Albion and Torquay United, he joined Rovers for £10 in June 1930 and missed a penalty against Northampton Town on his club debut. He was to play for Rovers in nine league matches, his only goal was a penalty against Gillingham. He left for Walsall in 1931, but died in 1940 at the age of 35, leaving a widow and nine children aged nine and under.

SATURDAY 2nd FEBRUARY 1957

One of the most iconic images of Rovers' halcyon days in the 1950s is that of Jackie Pitt and Bristol City's Ernie Peacock leaving the field of play arm-in-arm after both men had been sent off for fighting in a typically tumultuous local derby. The Third Division (South) game at Eastville ended goalless, but is remembered for this incident in which two of the hard men of 1950s Bristolian football – both with long loyal careers with their club – enjoyed their moment in the public eye.

TUESDAY 3rd FEBRUARY 1885

Archie Hughes was born in Neilston, a small town in Renfrewshire. Formerly with Manchester City, Bury and Millwall, Archibald Morris Hughes joined Rovers from Exeter City in February 1911 and played for the club in 34 Southern League matches, scoring five goals. One of his goals was Rovers' third in the comprehensive 5-1 victory at Southampton on his debut, whilst he also added one of the six through which New Brompton were defeated later that season.

SATURDAY 4th FEBRUARY 1922

Bill Panes has the dubious distinction of being the first Bristol Rovers player sent off in a Football League match. Rovers defeated Luton Town 2-0 at Eastville, yet the talking point was clearly the dismissal of full-back Panes for a foul on Luton's Australian-born inside-right Henry Higginbotham. A 'usually inoffensive man' (*Western Daily Press*), Panes had responded to provocation ten minutes after half-time and struck his opponent in the face. Referee Mr Tolfree of Southampton had little option but to send him from the field.

SATURDAY 5TH FEBRUARY 1955

Six goals in 41 minutes is an impressive tally and this was the second-half contribution of Blackburn Rovers' Tommy Briggs, whose seven goals helped destroy Rovers 8-3 at Ewood Park. Rovers had led 3-2 at the interval, with Bill Roost and Vic Lambden (twice) giving Rovers leads cancelled out first by Eddie Crossan, and then by seven-goal Briggs, who set a club goalscoring record in the process as well as hitting a post. His six shots and a header helped consign Rovers to their heaviest league defeat since 1936.

SATURDAY 5TH FEBRUARY 2005

Grimsby Town's Stacey Coldicott wore three different numbers on his back in the opening nine minutes of his side's 3-0 defeat at the Memorial Stadium. Twice succumbing to facial injuries, he had to change his shirt and so wore numbers 11, 27 and 20. The match proved to be an easy victory for Rovers. The Memorial Stadium crowd of 6,134 was treated to three first-half goals, with James Hunt, Ryan Williams and Richard Walker all scoring in a 17-minute spell.

TUESDAY 6TH FEBRUARY 1962

Jeff Meacham, a Bristol Rovers forward in the late 1980s, was born in Bristol. Already a veteran of the local football scene, he played for many non-league sides in the Bristol area over two decades and was with Rovers, his sole Football League club, from March 1987 until he joined Weymouth in August 1988. In total, he started 19 league games for Rovers and was used as a substitute in seven more; all nine of his league goals were scored at Twerton Park.

THURSDAY 7TH FEBRUARY 1952

An exciting 3-3 draw with Orient at Eastville was preceded by a one-minute silence to remember the life of King George VI, who had died 24 hours earlier. There were 10,000 spectators at Eastville and they witnessed two goals from the prolific Geoff Bradford as well as an own goal from Orient wing-half Jackie Deverall; Les Blizzard, Dennis Pacey and Tom Harris scored for the visitors.

SATURDAY 7TH FEBRUARY 2004

Magno Silva Vieira became the first Brazilian to score against Bristol Rovers. On loan from Wigan Athletic, he scored the first goal of his professional career after 31 minutes of Northampton Town's 2-0 victory over Rovers at the Sixfields Stadium, after goalkeeper Kevin Miller had missed a loose ball. He later scored from a header in November 2004, 19 minutes into extra time. The goal, for Carlisle United – then a non-league side – knocked Rovers out of the FA Cup.

SATURDAY 8TH FEBRUARY 1930

The first of only five Rovers players to have scored for both clubs in a league fixture was John Hamilton. The Scottish wing-half contrived to score at both ends as Rovers lost 3-2 to Newport County at Eastville, with top scorer Jack Phillips adding the home side's other strike. Hamilton, in fact, only scored two goals at the right end in his 63 league games for the club between 1929 and 1931.

WEDNESDAY 9TH FEBRUARY 1898

Frank Wragge, who was born in Wolverhampton, was a rugged centre-back, strong in the air and tough in the tackle. A May 1923 signing from the Midlands side Oakengates Town, he played in 62 league matches for Rovers over three seasons, scoring once in a fixture against Swindon Town in September 1925. He later won a Birmingham and District League championship with Stafford Rangers, played in Torquay United's first-ever Football League match and ended his professional career playing for Walsall against Rovers. He died in Shrewsbury in 1973 at the age of 75.

THURSDAY 10TH FEBRUARY 1923

After only 30 minutes of a Third Division (South) game at Eastville, Luton Town's goalkeeper Tom Gibbon left the field with an injury. At this point, Jerry Morgan had already scored for Rovers and the score was 1-1. Outside-right Sid Hoar went in goal and Rovers contrived to fail to score against the stand-in, with the match finishing 1-1 before a 9,000 crowd. The chief culprit was centre-half Jock Rutherford who, when Rovers were awarded a second-half penalty, shot wide of the post.

SATURDAY 10TH FEBRUARY 1990

In four league games and one FA Cup tie played on artificial surfaces, Rovers were victorious only once. David Mehew scored the only goal of the game at Deepdale, as Rovers defeated Preston North End 1-0 en route to the Third Division championship. This game was played before a crowd of 5,956.

SATURDAY 11TH FEBRUARY 1893

Rovers recorded a 2-1 win at home to Bristol St George in front of a crowd described in the local press as "very good". There was torrential rain throughout the second half, but Rovers held out for the victory afforded by goals from 23-year-old centre-forward Charlie Beverley and the more experienced inside-left Bill Rogers. Rovers were captained by their right-back Claude Hodgson, a shoemaker who had represented Gloucestershire on six occasions and was to play in 82 matches for Rovers, scoring twice.

TUESDAY 11TH FEBRUARY 1992

In the FA Cup, Rovers had earned a plum home game with Liverpool. A then Twerton Park record of 9,484 had watched a thrilling 1-1 draw with players called Saunders scoring for both clubs. Dean Saunders, however, hit the headlines after receiving a three-match ban for elbowing Ian Alexander, an offence missed by the referee but captured by television cameras. Extraordinarily, in the replay, Carl Saunders' powerful long-range right-foot volley gave Rovers an interval lead at Anfield but, before a 30,142 crowd, Liverpool won 2-1 through goals from Steve McManaman and Dean Saunders. The Reds progressed to beat Sunderland in the final.

SATURDAY 12TH FEBRUARY 1927

Second-half goals from Joe Clennell and Bill Culley earned Rovers a 2-0 victory over Brentford before a 10,000 crowd at Griffin Park.

SATURDAY 12TH FEBRUARY 1972

Bill Stoddart's death in Lanchester, County Durham at the age of 64 marked the passing of a fine centre-half who represented Rovers in 40 league games between 1931 and 1933. Born near Durham in October 1907, he also played league football for Coventry City, Southampton and Accrington Stanley, for whom he played in their largest ever league defeat, a 9-0 thrashing by Barnsley in February 1934. He was also noted for his exceptionally long throw-ins.

THURSDAY 13TH FEBRUARY 1997

The West Stand at the Memorial Stadium was officially opened for a rugby game between Bristol and Auckland Blues. The stand, which could hold almost 1,500 people, had cost £2,000,000 and was given a second opening two days later when Rovers beat Luton Town 3-2 in Division Two.

SATURDAY 14TH FEBRUARY 2009

High-flying Scunthorpe United were defeated 2-0 on their own pitch by a resurgent Rovers side that was missing injured top scorer Rickie Lambert. Not to be outdone, the two strikers, Darryl Duffy and Jo Kuffour, both scored before half-time, whilst goalkeeper Steve Phillips saved a second-half penalty from Paul Hayes, given for handball against Craig Hinton. Four days later, Rovers secured their first-ever league win against Yeovil Town, by a comfortable 3-0 margin.

SATURDAY 15TH FEBRUARY 1919

Full-back Bill Panes never scored a league goal for Rovers, but he did score a hat-trick in a wartime game against Great Western Railway. Mind you, most players scored that day, including regular goalkeeper Bill Grubb, who also scored three times. Edward Rawlings notched four, Ellis Crompton and Len Gyles three each, Harry Roe twice and Bert Bennett and Percy Whitton one apiece. Rovers' 20-0 victory remains their highest in any fixture.

SATURDAY 15TH FEBRUARY 1958

Supporters of football in Bristol could not believe their luck as Rovers and City were drawn together in the fifth round of the FA Cup. An attendance of 39,126 at Ashton Gate brought gate receipts of £5,439 and witnessed arguably the most exciting of all Bristol derby matches: seven goals, a missed penalty and a highly controversial Geoff Bradford winner seven minutes from time. Rovers should have taken a first-minute lead, but it was Barry Watkins who scored against his former club three minutes later to give City an early lead. By half-time Norman Sykes, Dai Ward and Barrie Meyer had scored, Ron Nicholls had saved a penalty from Watkins and Rovers led 3-1. However, City recovered to level at 3-3 and, with a quarter-final place up for grabs, Ward's through ball to Bradford, looking suspiciously offside, brought Rovers a 4-3 victory.

JO KUFFOUR HELPED ROVERS TOPPLE HIGH-FLYING SCUNTHORPE IN FEBRUARY 2009

SATURDAY 16TH FEBRUARY 1985

Les Berry, a Rovers goalkeeper and a cricketer of some renown, died in Leicestershire at the age of 78. Tall and agile, Berry played in 34 league games for Rovers during the 1930-31 season, even though he had conceded a hat-trick to Northampton Town's Ted Bowen on his debut. He also scored over 30,000 runs in his first-class cricket career between 1924 and 1951, in which he captained Leicestershire. The summer he joined Rovers he had scored 232 against Sussex at Leicester.

SATURDAY 16TH FEBRUARY 2008

Live on terrestrial television, Rovers defeated Southampton, a team one division higher, in the fifth round of the FA Cup to reach the quarter-finals for only the third time. A crowd of 11,920 at the Memorial Stadium saw Rickie Lambert, who had earlier had an effort ruled out, crash the ball home with only six minutes remaining to secure Rovers' progression to the last eight.

SATURDAY 17TH FEBRUARY 1996

Rotherham United's goalkeeper Matthew Clarke left the field injured at half-time of a league match against Rovers before a crowd of 5,412. Within seconds of the restart, Marcus Stewart had scored past full-back Gary Bowyer, who had valiantly stepped into the goalkeeper's position, but this proved to be the only goal of the game.

FRIDAY 18TH FEBRUARY 1910

Lance Carr, the first black player to appear for Rovers, was born in Johannesburg, the son of a professional athlete. Formerly at Liverpool and Newport County, he played 42 times for Rovers in the 1946-47 season, scoring eight times, before joining Merthyr Town on a free transfer. He died in Greenwich in April 1983.

SATURDAY 18TH FEBRUARY 1984

Both Rovers and Walsall fielded their player-managers for a Third Division fixture and both scored in Rovers' 4-2 victory at Eastville in front of 5,643 spectators. David Williams, Rovers' player-manager, scored Rovers' second goal, with Paul Bannon and Paul Randall also scoring, along with an own goal. The Saddlers player-boss Alan Buckley scored one of the visitors' two goals.

FRIDAY 19TH FEBRUARY 1886

Eight miners were killed and 13 seriously injured in a gas explosion at Easton mine, one of several coal mines that provided employment in Victorian times around the Eastville area. Rovers' players and supporters relied heavily on the coalmining industry for their incomes. Among the dead were a father and son in George and Henry Bennett; one of the victims left eight young children. Dr. W. G. Grace, the England cricketer, tended to the injured. The manager of the mine, William Boult Monks, never fully recovered from the shock and threw himself down the mine to his death in March 1892.

TUESDAY 20TH FEBRUARY 1996

Some records credit Justin Channing with two own goals in the 3-2 defeat at Wrexham; if this is true, he would be the only Rovers player to have suffered such a fate. In front of a crowd of 3,235, Channing deflected home Hunter's header after 25 minutes, then turned Peter Ward's cross into his own net 30 minutes later. Most records give one own goal to Channing, with Barry Hunter and Lee Jones also scoring for Wrexham while Peter Beadle and Andy Tillson contributed with Rovers' goals.

WEDNESDAY 21ST FEBRUARY 1923

Between 1921 and 1927, Rovers played Third Division (South) matches against Aberdare Athletic, until the South Wales side lost its league status and was replaced by Torquay United. When Rovers played at the Athletic Ground in February 1923, the referee mistakenly blew five minutes early for full time with the game scoreless. After a linesman pointed out the mistake, the sides returned to play out the remaining minutes, though no goals were forthcoming.

SATURDAY 22ND FEBRUARY 1902

Ted Smith was born in Sunderland, where he worked in the dockyards before embarking on a football career that took him to Hartlepool, Newport County, Portsmouth, Reading and Luton Town before he signed for Rovers from Preston North End in September 1931. A powerfully-built left-back, he replaced Frank Hill in Rovers' side and played in eight league games before an injury ended his career. He later worked in the car industry and died in Luton in March 1972.

SATURDAY 23RD FEBRUARY 1907

A powerful Arsenal side defeated Rovers 1-0 in the FA Cup at Highbury. David Neave scored the only goal 20 minutes after half-time, at a time when Rovers were down to ten men, with captain Dick Pudan receiving treatment after a crunching challenge from the England international Tim Coleman. The Arsenal side included Willy Garbutt, who was later coach at Genoa, Roma, Napoli and Athletic Bilbao; 'Mister English' was the first professional manager in Italy, a charismatic visionary and legendary pipe smoker, who led Genoa to three championship titles, the most recent coming in 1924.

SATURDAY 24TH FEBRUARY 1934

Captain Albert Prince-Cox, the charismatic Rovers manager, was involved in flying a group of Rovers supporters to Cardiff to watch a league game. Those involved paid eight shillings each for a ticket from Whitchurch Airport and the scheme aroused a good deal of publicity in the national press. Stand tickets at Ninian Park cost two shillings and six pence each and Rovers won the game 5-1, with Jack Havelock scoring twice. In a similar scheme, Rovers players and supporters flew to Norwich in September 2004 for a League Cup tie that was lost 1-0.

SATURDAY 24TH FEBRUARY 1951

Rovers ground out a goalless draw with Newcastle United in the FA Cup quarter-final at St. James' Park. It was the first of only three occasions that the club had progressed so far in this tournament. The attendance at the fixture, 62,787, which produced £7,561 in gate receipts, remains the largest ever at a football match involving Bristol Rovers. Around 5,000 Rovers supporters had witnessed this momentous match, but some 100,000 queued at Eastville for tickets for the Wednesday afternoon replay, which was lost 3-1.

SATURDAY 24TH FEBRUARY 1962

Despite being the first occasion that a club had flown its team to a Football League match Preston North End's visit to Eastville, watched by 10,601, proved to be a fruitless journey. Goals from Rovers' Peter Hooper and Bobby Jones ensured a 2-1 victory. Alfie Biggs, who had already made his name with Rovers, scored Preston's goal.

SATURDAY 25TH FEBRUARY 1928

Rovers gave a league debut to 15-year-old Ronnie Dix in the 2-1 home victory over Charlton Athletic. He became the youngest player ever to represent the club in the Football League, appearing before a crowd of 8,000 at Eastville in a match won through two Arthur Ormston goals. Seven days later, Dix scored one of Rovers' goals in a 3-0 win against Norwich City to set a record that stands to this day as the youngest Football League goalscorer for any club.

SATURDAY 26TH FEBRUARY 1921

Though they had conceded a penalty in only their second Football League fixture, it took 28 matches for Rovers to be awarded one of their own. It was successfully converted by centre-forward Sid Leigh at Vicarage Road. Rovers lost 2-1 before a crowd of 6,000.

SUNDAY 27TH FEBRUARY 1898

John Stevenson, who scored once in seven league matches for Rovers in the 1932-33 season, was born in Wigan, the son of a Sunderland player. Previously with Ayr United, Aberdeen and Beith north of the border, he had joined Bury in time to help the Gigg Lane side secure the Second Division championship title in 1924. He also played in Division One before representing two Third Division (North) sides, Nelson and Carlisle United. Stevenson signed for Rovers in February 1933 and played in six consecutive games in which Rovers were unbeaten, scoring against Orient. He later played for Falkirk and died in Carlisle in March 1979.

MONDAY 27TH FEBRUARY 1989

Wimbledon's defensive midfielder Ian Hazel joined Rovers on a month's loan ahead of the game against Reading. Born in London in December 1967, Hazel's Wimbledon debut had been against Liverpool and, signing full professional forms with Rovers in the summer of 1989, he was to play in seven (plus ten as substitute) league matches before leaving in the spring of 1992. After a loan spell at Gloucester City, he played for Maidstone United and Slough Town, before embarking on a long career around the Surrey area, eventually serving as manager at Molesey, Walton & Hersham, Sutton United and Leatherhead.

WEDNESDAY 28TH FEBRUARY 1951

Astonishingly, lower-league Rovers had held mighty Newcastle United to a goalless draw at St. James' Park in the FA Cup quarter-final, so 30,074 joyous spectators crammed into Eastville for the replay. Fifteen minutes in, amid scenes of incredulous delight, Geoff Bradford scored a fine opportunist goal to give Rovers a surprise lead, prompting strains of the crowd's favourite song, Goodnight Irene, to echo around the ground. By half-time, however, goals from Ernie Taylor, whose shot deflected in off Geoff Fox, Charlie Crowe and the legendary Jackie Milburn gave the Magpies victory, despite a spirited second-half Rovers revival. Newcastle United went on to win the cup, the same eleven players who had faced Rovers twice in four days defeating Blackpool at Wembley.

FRIDAY 28TH FEBRUARY 1992

Rovers' worst loss since February 1987 came at the Abbey Stadium on a Friday evening. Cambridge United, who scored four goals in an eleven-minute second-half spell after half-time, went second in the table by beating Rovers 6-1 in front of a crowd of 6,164, with five opponents scoring. Neil Heaney became only the third opponent to score for both sides in a league game and for the first time against Rovers both the opposition's substitutes scored. One of these subs was John Taylor, later United's all-time top goalscorer, and a Rovers player from 1992 to 1994.

SATURDAY 29TH FEBRUARY 1936

Only on two occasions have Rovers played league matches on this date. In 1936, Rovers defeated Millwall 2-0 in front of a 5,000 crowd at Eastville, with Jack Woodman and Stan Prout scoring the goals. In 1964 Rovers won narrowly, with Bobby Jones scoring the only goal of the game, before a 6,061 crowd at Shrewsbury Town's Gay Meadow. Charles Heinemann, a Rovers forward in 1925-26, was born on 29th February 1904, whilst Billy Compton, an outside-left who played for Rovers in 1928-29, died on 29th February 1976.

BRISTOL ROVERS
On This Day

MARCH

SATURDAY 1st MARCH 1930

Ted Purdon, a strikingly blond centre-forward who played in four league matches for Rovers in 1960-61, scoring once against Luton Town, was born in Johannesburg. Having arrived in the United Kingdom as part of the Maritz Brothers FC 1950 tour, Purdon enjoyed a successful league career with Birmingham City, Sunderland, Workington and Barrow, before signing for Rovers in September 1960. He later emigrated to Canada, became a successful businessman and died in Toronto in April 2007.

WEDNESDAY 2nd MARCH 1988

Only five Rovers players have managed to score for both sides in the same league fixture, the fourth such example being central defender Geoff Twentyman, who contributed both the goals as Rovers drew 1-1 with Notts County at Twerton Park. He scored six times for Rovers in 148 league matches – plus four as substitute – for Rovers between 1986 and 1993 before embarking on a successful career in local radio. More recently, Byron Anthony scored for both sides against Nottingham Forest in September 2007.

SATURDAY 3rd MARCH 1990

During Rovers' decade in exile in Bath, the largest league win was the 6-1 victory over Wigan Athletic, in which Carl Saunders, a recent signing from Stoke City to replace Gary Penrice, scored the first league hat-trick seen at Twerton Park. This was the Latics' record league defeat, eclipsing the 5-0 loss suffered when Rovers visited Springfield Park in February 1983. There were 5,169 spectators at this Third Division game and Rovers' other goals were scored by David Mehew, Ian Alexander and Ian Holloway.

SATURDAY 4th MARCH 1961

Two Peter Hooper goals earned Rovers a 2-1 victory at Lincoln City, in front of a crowd of 15,006 at Sincil Bank. Andy Graver scored for the Imps. This was one of the last whispers of success for some years, as the great side of the 1950s was retiring or moving on. Within years, Rovers had dropped to Division Three and were struggling to prevent relegation to the basement tier. It would be September 1981 before Rovers and Lincoln next crossed swords in the Football League.

THURSDAY 5TH MARCH 1739

Coal mining was arguably the major source of employment around the Eastville area over the two centuries leading up to Rovers' formation. The Reverend George Whitefield, the celebrated Methodist preacher who co-wrote Hark! The Herald Angels Sing, recorded meeting 2,000 colliers at Fishponds. The shallow mines in this area produced a great deal of coal, up to a thousand tons per day by the late Victorian era.

SATURDAY 6TH MARCH 1982

Central defender Tim Parkin contrived to score for both clubs as Rovers crashed to a 5-2 defeat away to Swindon Town in front of a crowd of 6,689. The future Rovers midfielder Roy Carter converted a penalty for Town, Charlie Henry scored and there were also two goals for Paul Rideout, scorer of Everton's winning goal in the 1995 FA Cup Final. Archie Stephens was Rovers' other scorer.

TUESDAY 6TH MARCH 2007

The first time that Rovers faced a Benin international in the opposition was in the 1-1 draw at Accrington Stanley. Romuald Boco, though born in France, had represented the African nation on 17 occasions. Before a crowd of only 1,302, Rovers took a 58th minute lead through Richard Walker before Shaun Whalley equalised in injury time.

SATURDAY 7TH MARCH 1936

What is striking about Rovers' 2-0 defeat at Torquay United is that Rovers players scored both the goals. Jack Preece and Allan Murray both contrived to score first-half own goals past goalkeeper Jack Ellis in front of a low crowd of 2,128 at Plainmoor. The only other league game when two Rovers players scored own goals was another 2-0 defeat, when Peter Sampson and Norman Sykes both conceded own goals in a defeat at Stoke City in January 1962.

MONDAY 7TH MARCH 1977

The first ex-Rovers player to play at the new Wembley, Graeme Power, was born in Harrow. He played in 25 (plus one as substitute) league games for Rovers at left-back between 1996 and 1998 before playing at the national stadium with Truro City.

THURSDAY 8TH MARCH 1906

Joe Nicholls, a six-foot-four-inches-tall goalkeeper who played for Rovers between 1936 and 1939, was born in Nottingham. A former Grenadier Guard who had enjoyed an international trial during a decade with Spurs, he played in 112 league matches for Rovers, missing only one league or cup game from January 1937 to the outbreak of World War II. Joe Nicholls died in Nottingham in June 1973, at the age of 67.

MONDAY 9TH MARCH 1908

The Rovers goalkeeper Foster Windsor was born in Bristol. A product of the local football scene, Windsor played in 20 league matches for Rovers between 1932 and 1934, when he moved on to Bath City and later Warminster Town. A darts champion and keen angler, he lived in Bristol and died there in March 1985, shortly after his 72nd birthday.

SUNDAY 9TH MARCH 2008

Having played Newcastle United in 1951 and Fulham in 1958, Rovers faced West Bromwich Albion in the club's third FA Cup quarter-final. Playing at home to second-tier Albion, and as only one top tier side was still in the competition, Rovers believed progression to the semi-finals was a real possibility. However, a bumper crowd of 12,011, which set a new ground record at The Memorial Stadium, saw Albion run away with a 5-1 victory. After James Morrison's opener on 16 minutes, Ishmael Miller netted three times; on 30, 69 and 85 minutes. Danny Coles' goal after 31 minutes was all Rovers had to cheer.

SATURDAY 10TH MARCH 2007

Defeat at Boston United, where Albert Jarrett was allowed to score twice in the opening nine minutes, left Rovers in 16th place in League One. This game marked the Rovers debut of Joe Jacobson, the first British Jew to play in the Football League since Crewe Alexandra's Barry Silkman in 1986. Incredibly, rising from 16th place, Rovers were promoted at the end of the season. Following the York Street loss, Rovers won eight and drew two of their remaining eleven league matches to creep into a play-off spot, from where they defeated Lincoln City over two legs and Shrewsbury Town at Wembley.

SATURDAY 11TH MARCH 1905

Southampton came to Eastville for what became effectively a Southern League championship decider. It was bizarre that, for the second consecutive season, a crunch fixture between Rovers and the Saints ended 6-1 to the home side. Fred Harrison gave the Saints a 20th-minute advantage before a 10,000 crowd, but two goals in a minute gave the home side a half-time lead, after which Billy Beats, Rovers' former England international, burst through for a solo goal. He then added another with his head. As Rovers piled on the agony for the visitors, two goals in the final 20 minutes left the home side clear favourites for the championship, which they later secured. Billy Clark, Hill Griffiths, Jack Lewis and Bill Hales all scored for Rovers.

TUESDAY 11TH MARCH 1969

A run of four consecutive league defeats was arrested by a 1-1 draw at home to Torquay United in front of an Eastville crowd of 7,433. Phil Sandercock, the young Torquay defender, turned the ball into his own net to become, at 18 years 39 days, the youngest own goal scorer to register a goal in Rovers' favour in the league. John Rudge – who was to score 17 goals for Rovers in 50 (plus 20 as substitute) league games between the spring of 1972 and 1975 – scored Torquay's goal.

SATURDAY 11TH MARCH 2000

A mediocre crowd of 4,049 at Gigg Lane witnessed Rovers battle out the goalless draw that took them back to the top of the table with eleven games remaining. Promotion, surely, was now a certainty. When the next game was won, 3-1 at home to Rotherham United, supporters believed even more fervently that Rovers were about to return to the second tier of English football, but a terrible run of one win in the final ten games saw that dream vanish and Rovers plummeted through the play-offs, which they missed out on by dint of losing at already-relegated Cardiff City on the final day of a hugely demoralising season. Twelve months later, Rovers were relegated to the basement division for the first time in the club's history.

SATURDAY 12TH MARCH 1955

As if any trip to Elland Road were not difficult enough, Rovers conceded a goal after just eleven seconds, the fastest goal from the kick-off in any game featuring Rovers down the years. Leeds United's inside-left Bobby Forrest scored the opening strike and Rovers, though avoiding a heavy defeat, lost this Second Division fixture 2-0, with Harold Brook notching the second goal in front of a crowd of 16,922.

SATURDAY 12TH MARCH 1977

Ian Holloway became the first player at any club in the country to be signed on as an associate schoolboy. The regulations had recently changed and were to be implemented from that day; Rovers signed the promising youngster on his 14th birthday. Ian Holloway went on to spend many years at Rovers, appearing in almost 400 league games in three spells before enjoying a stint as club manager.

SATURDAY 13TH MARCH 1920

Five minutes from time, trying to stop the ball as it flew out of the ground, one unfortunate spectator fell headlong into the River Frome, emerging uninjured but with his pride bruised. Rovers defeated Norwich City 5-3 in this Southern League match, with the Canaries' George Dexter, in his only first-class match, and Rovers' Tom Brandon both conceding own goals.

THURSDAY 14TH MARCH 1929

When Rovers won 2-1 at Charlton Athletic, all three goals were scored by the home side. Rovers were behind in the first minute, when Wilson Lennox, who later spent many years coaching in Holland, gave the home side the lead in front of a crowd of 10,000 at The Valley. However, two Addicks defenders, Norman Smith and Albert Langford, contrived to concede own goals and hand Rovers victory in this Third Division (South) match.

SATURDAY 14TH MARCH 1886

Eastville Rovers hosted Right and Might on The Downs in a game restricted to one hour in length, using tapes for crossbars. Fred Churchill led the line and the Perrin brothers, Bill and Walter, both played, but the match finished goalless.

IAN HOLLOWAY BECAME THE FIRST EVER ASSOCIATE SCHOOLBOY WHEN HE SIGNED FOR ROVERS IN MAY 1977

SATURDAY 14TH MARCH 1936

Ray Warren made his league debut for Rovers in the home defeat against Queens Park Rangers; although he played at inside-forward, he was to make his name as a reliable wing-half. His final league game for the club came in December 1955, giving him a league career with the club spanning 19 years 288 days. This career is more than three years longer than any other Rovers player, Wally McArthur and George Petherbridge being the only two other players whose careers spanned more than 15 years.

SATURDAY 15TH MARCH 1891

Rovers lost 2-0 at Bristol St. George in a friendly. Centre-forward Fred Yates was unable to add to his impressive goal tally for the club, whilst goalkeeper Edward Tucker conceded a goal in each half.

SATURDAY 15TH MARCH 1884

The earliest available line-up for a Rovers fixture was when the Black Arabs, as they were then known, lost away to Right and Might to a single goal a minute after half-time. "Right and Might won the toss and kicked down the hill", reported the local press. Rovers fielded H. Griffiths in goal, Bill Miller and Bill Pepperell at full-back, a half-back line of Bill Braund, Jack Miller and captain Henry Martin, with five forwards in Richard Conyers, Fred Channing, Bill Davies, Fred Hall and Harry Horsey.

SATURDAY 15TH MARCH 1947

Antonio Gallego, a Spanish Civil War refugee, played in only one Football League game and it was for Norwich City against Rovers in the Third Division (South) in front of a crowd of 18,051 at Carrow Road. An exciting game finished 3-3, with Ken Wookey, Len Hodges and Lance Carr grabbing the Rovers goals.

MONDAY 15TH MARCH 1993

The appointment of John Ward as Rovers manager marked the starting-point in rebuilding a side capable of pushing for promotion from the third tier of English football. Ward, born in Lincoln in April 1951, was to re-establish Rovers as a progressive side in that division and took the club to a play-off final at Wembley in 1995. He remained at the helm until May 1996.

WEDNESDAY 16TH MARCH 1927

Not every week does a team throw away a three-goal lead and lose the game. Rovers led 3-0 at Crystal Palace after just 17 minutes before a crowd of 5,347, but were outplayed from then on. By half-time, Rovers led 4-2, but Palace stormed back to win an exciting game 7-4, with Percy Cherrett completing a second-half hat-trick. Bill Culley scored twice for Rovers, with Jack Rowley and Tom Williams adding a goal apiece. This remains the only occasion in league football that Rovers have led by three goals and lost the match.

TUESDAY 16TH MARCH 1982

The only occasion Bristol Rovers have been deducted league points followed the 1-1 draw at Newport County's Somerton Park. In front of a crowd of 5,312, County's Tommy Tynan and Rovers' Brian Williams had exchanged penalty kicks. A clerical mix-up meant that teenager Steve Bailey played in this game, though his professional forms did not reach the league headquarters until after the match. In line with league rules, Rovers were docked the points for having fielded an ineligible player. The club would have only finished one place higher if they hadn't been docked the points.

WEDNESDAY 17TH MARCH 1937

Billy Clark died in Bristol at the age of 56. Born in Airdrie early in the palindrome year of 1881, he joined Rovers from Port Glasgow Athletic in May 1904 and played for the club in 133 Southern League matches, scoring 35 goals and winning a Southern League championship medal in 1904-05. Later a First Division player from April 1908 with Sunderland and Bristol City, and a Second Division forward at Leicester Fosse, Clark retired in 1912 and took over as proprietor of the Clifton Wood Wine and Spirit Vaults in Bristol.

SATURDAY 18TH MARCH 1933

The former Rovers forward Chris Ball was sent off by referee Bert Mee of Mansfield, whilst playing for Walsall against Crewe Alexandra. Nothing particularly odd about this statement, you might think. Twelve months earlier, though, Ball had again been sent off and once more it was by referee Bert Mee, whilst playing for Walsall against Crewe Alexandra.

MONDAY 18TH MARCH 1940

Tony Gough, who was born in Bath, held the extraordinary record of having played league football in the 1950s and 1970s, without having done so in the 1960s. As a teenage inside-forward, he played in Rovers' 2-1 victory over Sheffield Wednesday in April 1959 and was to appear for both Swindon Town and Torquay United after a decade with Bath City. Later Hereford United's captain when they famously defeated Newcastle United in the FA Cup in 1972, Gough appeared in a club record 481 games for Bath City.

MONDAY 19TH MARCH 1973

One of the most spectacular collapses in Rovers' league history came at Walsall where Rovers led 3-1 with 15 minutes to go in a Third Division fixture. In front of a crowd of 4,595, Rovers had scored through Bruce Bannister and Alan Warboys (2) after Bobby Shinton's ninth-minute goal had put the Saddlers ahead at half-time. Then there was a bomb scare and the players were taken from the pitch for their safety. The remaining minutes were played out with Walsall scoring three times to secure a 4-3 victory, with Chris Jones' second goal of the night and Barnie Wright's headed winner both coming in the seven minutes of added time awarded by referee Jim Whalley of Southport.

MONDAY 20TH MARCH 1961

Geoff Bradford, Bobby Jones, Doug Hillard and Peter Hooper enthralled the 15,699 Eastville crowd with goals in a 4-2 Second Division win over Southampton. One of the Saints' goals was scored by Terry Paine, who was on the verge of a successful career. He was to score for Hereford United against Rovers in April 1977, just over 16 years later. No other opponent has scored league goals against the club more than 16 years apart.

SUNDAY 21ST MARCH 1909

Whilst many clubs play overseas on a regular basis, Rovers' first overseas game came in Paris, where Rovers and Southampton drew 5-5 in a charity game. This fixture was fulfilled under floodlights and attracted a good deal of attention from the French media as the game had barely taken off yet across the channel. Two goals to one ahead at half-time, Rovers drew 5-5 with Fred Corbett scoring three times and Walter Gerrish and Gilbert Ovens claiming a goal apiece.

SATURDAY 22ND MARCH 1958

When Orient played at Eastville, both sides missed penalties, with Rovers' Peter Hooper, and the visitors' John Hartburn both wasting opportunities to score. Rovers were less bothered about the miss, because they won 4-0 anyway. An Eastville crowd of 15,533 was able to cheer two goals from Barrie Meyer, later a Test match umpire at cricket, and one each from John McIlvenny and Peter Hooper.

SATURDAY 23RD MARCH 1895

St. George Football Club was a major force in Victorian football around the Bristol area and their success reached a pinnacle in the 1894-95 season when they swept all before them en route to the Western League championship. By the end of March, when they were due to play Rovers, the side was still undefeated all season. That proud run came to an inglorious end as they lost 2-0 to Rovers on their own pitch. Bob Horsey and Bill Rogers scored Rovers' goals.

WEDNESDAY 23RD MARCH 1927

In severe wind and rain, Rovers and Gillingham agreed to forfeit their half-time interval and play on. Gillingham, who fielded the future Rovers left-back Bill Pickering, were able to benefit from a Jimmy Hayden own goal and won this Third Division (South) fixture 2-0. A very brave 2,500 spectators witnessed inside-left Bill Arblaster also get his name on the score-sheet.

SATURDAY 24TH MARCH 1888

The Gloucestershire XI that lost 1-0 to Wiltshire contained seven Eastville Rovers players, Edward Tucker, George Friend, Herbert Rayner and four Bills (Somerton, Rogers, Taylor and Bush).

SATURDAY 24TH MARCH 1951

Rovers' goalless draw at Plymouth Argyle was the club's thousandth game in the Football League. There was a crowd of 21,066 at Home Park but, though Rovers had defeated Reading 4-0 in their previous fixture seven days earlier, the Argyle defence proved too stubborn to break down. Prior to kick-off Rovers had been forced into one change to their side and, with Bryan Bush unfit to play, the ever reliable George Petherbridge was recalled at outside-right.

SATURDAY 25TH MARCH 1989

Born on this day in Bath, Scott Sinclair became the second-youngest Rovers player in the Football League when he played against Orient in a 1-1 draw on Boxing Day 2004, aged 15. Only Ronnie Dix, back in 1928, had represented the club earlier, whilst only two other players – Simon Bryant and Neil Slatter – had played for Rovers in the league at the age of 16. A quick striker, Sinclair was 15 years 256 days old when he made his debut but, within six months, had left Rovers to join Chelsea.

FRIDAY 26TH MARCH 1897

Having been formed as Black Arabs and later having taken on the name Eastville Rovers, it was under the latter name that the club became a limited company. The advent of professionalism and the increased financial stakes involved in football had led the club to this position. The new ground at Eastville was about to be opened and the club strode on, taking on the name Bristol Rovers in February 1899.

TUESDAY 27TH MARCH 1948

Penalties were the order of the day at Eastville. Jackie Pitt became only the second player to score two penalties in a league game and his two early strikes, after just five and six minutes, gave the home crowd of 13,292 plenty to cheer. Undeterred, though, Newport County responded with a penalty after 33 minutes, converted by Len Emmanuel, whose nephew Gary Emmanuel was to play for Rovers between January 1979 and the summer of 1981. County, who featured two former Rovers players in Doug Hayward and Idris Lewis, recovered to win 3-2 with Bryn Allen scoring twice.

SATURDAY 28TH MARCH 1896

Herbert Edwin Smith, a Bedminster player, died overnight of head injuries sustained in a match against Rovers at Greenway Bush Lane, which Rovers won through a Richard Osborne goal. There had been a clash of heads, during the Gloucestershire Cup tie, and both Smith and Rovers' Fred Lovett had collapsed to the floor. Smith had twice returned to the pitch but was unable to complete the match. Sadly for Smith, he died at about 6am the following morning.

MONDAY 28TH MARCH 1932

A disastrous Easter Monday defeat before a crowd of 2,830 at Plainmoor equalled Rovers' heaviest ever loss, at that time, in league football. Rovers were four goals down by half-time against a supposedly struggling Torquay United side and finally went down 8-1. Outside-left Bert Young scored Rovers' consolation goal near the final whistle, but not before Bill Clayson emphasised the gap between the sides with three goals of his own in the final four minutes, scoring four times in all.

WEDNESDAY 28TH MARCH 1990

A flying header after 58 minutes from David Mehew earned Rovers a slender victory before a crowd of 6,480 at home to Notts County in the first leg of the Leyland DAF Cup Southern Final. A staunch defensive display at Meadow Lane then earned Rovers a place in the final against Tranmere Rovers… and the club's first trip ever to Wembley.

MONDAY 29TH MARCH 1948

In defeating Aldershot 7-1 at Eastville, Rovers were primarily indebted to Vic Lambden. His four goals included the fastest hat-trick from the start of a league match by any Rovers player. He scored after one, eight and 15 minutes before adding his fourth goal in the second half. This remains one of only 14 occasions when a Rovers player has completed his hat-trick before half-time in a league fixture. In this instance, Jackie Pitt scored twice for Rovers and Barry Watkins also scored.

SATURDAY 29TH MARCH 2008

Wayne Andrews became, after Brian Cash, Ryan Morgan and Tony Obi, only the fourth Rovers player who did not complete his only league appearance in Rovers' colours. Signed as a potential answer to Rovers' goalscoring concerns, the striker made his debut in a goalless draw at Yeovil Town in a League One match and left the field after 17 minutes following a challenge with Terry Skiverton. Andrews never reappeared for Rovers though, within a year Skiverton, by now manager at Yeovil, had signed him for the Somerset club.

SATURDAY 30TH MARCH 1991

When Brian Parkin was sent off against Brighton & Hove Albion, defender Ian Alexander became an instant hero by deputising in goal and saving the resultant penalty from John Byrne. Rovers lost the game 3-1, in front of a crowd of 6,276 at Twerton Park – despite a goal from Andy Reece – whilst Byrne was to miss another penalty against Rovers 18 months later, while playing for Sunderland.

MONDAY 31ST MARCH 1924

It is faintly embarrassing to lose 2-0 to a side that does not have a recognised goalkeeper available. Griff James was a reserve left-half for Aberdare Athletic, but agreed, in a goalkeeping crisis, to don the gloves for Rovers' Third Division (South) match in South Wales. James was largely untroubled, as the visitors lost without a whimper. Before a 3,000 crowd, Rovers lost to second-half goals from Arthur Metcalf and Dick Burgess.

WEDNESDAY 31ST MARCH 2004

The former Rovers midfielder Vitalijs Astafjevs won his 100th international cap, captaining Latvia to a 1-0 victory over Slovenia in Celje. He had won his first full cap in August 1992, as a late substitute for Jurijs Popkovs in a goalless draw with Denmark and, to mark the occasion of becoming the first Latvian to reach a hundred caps, he was presented with a bouquet of flowers on the pitch prior to the game. Astafjevs played for Rovers in 88 – plus 22 as substitute – league matches, scoring 16 goals between 1999 and 2003.

BRISTOL ROVERS
On This Day

APRIL

SATURDAY 1st APRIL 2000

The Stoke City goalkeeper Gavin Ward was attacked by a disgruntled home supporter during their 3-3 draw with Rovers at the Memorial Stadium. A Football Association hearing that June gave Rovers a suspended sentence of two points docked and a £10,000 fine, to be implemented should any similar incident occur within twelve months. During the match, Peter Thorne became the first opponent to score a league hat-trick at the Memorial Stadium, though his goals proved not enough to earn his side a victory.

SUNDAY 1st APRIL 2007

Having reached the final of the Johnstone's Paint Trophy, Rovers played at the Millennium Stadium in Cardiff for the first time in the club's history. Reports indicated that there were 37,000 Rovers fans present in a crowd of 59,025, the fourth highest attendance at any game featuring Rovers. Doncaster Rovers were quickly out of the blocks, with Jonathan Forte scoring after just 38 seconds and Paul Heffernan adding a second only five minutes in. When all appeared lost, Rovers rallied and equalised through Richard Walker's penalty, and a Sammy Igoe shot, to take the tie into extra time. However, a Graeme Lee header from a corner after 110 minutes consigned Rovers to defeat. Nonetheless, this game acted as part of the springboard for Rovers' late season revival and, against the odds, the club was at Wembley the following month, to seal promotion through the play-offs.

MONDAY 2nd APRIL 1934

Despite recalling Doug Lewis and Jack Havelock, Rovers drew a league game 0-0 at Exeter City before a 10,000 crowd.

THURSDAY 2nd APRIL 1998

Ronnie Dix, the youngest Rovers player and an England international, died in Bristol at the age of 85. A Bristolian by birth, he had become the youngest goalscorer for any club in the Football League when he found the net against Norwich City in March 1928 and he contributed 33 goals in exactly 100 league matches with Rovers. Later at Blackburn Rovers, Aston Villa, Derby County and Spurs, he won one England cap, scoring against Norway in 1938, and turned out for Reading after World War II.

SATURDAY 3rd APRIL 1897

To mark the official opening of Eastville, Rovers invited the reigning league champions and FA Cup winners Aston Villa to play in a friendly. A crowd of 5,000 came to the ground and was rewarded with an open game of exciting football, which Villa won 5-0. The 16-acre site had been bought from the Smythe family of Ashton Court for £150, which Rovers then developed by spending a further £1,255 so that it could initially hold a crowd of 20,000.

TUESDAY 3rd APRIL 1984

Only the swift actions of Rovers' long-serving physiotherapist Roy Dolling saved the life of Rovers' Aiden McCaffrey, who had swallowed his tongue during an Associate Members' Cup-tie against Southend United. Rovers won the game 2-1, with Mark Hughes and Micky Adams scoring before a crowd of 1,480; Greg Shepherd scored for the Shrimpers. Astonishingly, this was the second time that Dolling had saved a player's life as he had also assisted Ian Alexander in a similar situation during an FA Cup tie at home to Fisher Athletic in November 1988.

FRIDAY 4th APRIL 1890

"An all-action player with something of a short temper", Tom Howarth was born in Rochdale; he also died there in September 1969 at the age of 79. A Rovers player in the 1922-23 season, he scored four goals in 21 appearances as a forward. His goal return was somewhat better at Bristol City and Leeds United and he scored for City in their 1920 FA Cup semi-final which was lost 2-1 to Huddersfield Town. He ended his career as a goalkeeper in the Western League, whilst his son Sid played for Swansea, Merthyr, Aston Villa and Walsall.

SATURDAY 5th APRIL 1952

Throughout a long career, Vic Lambden scored many goals for Rovers. However, he only once conceded an own goal and that was when he scored both the goals in a 1-1 draw away to Brighton & Hove Albion. The match at the Goldstone Ground was watched by an attendance of 14,268. Only three players have scored more league goals for Rovers than the 117 Lambden scored in his 268 appearances.

SATURDAY 6TH APRIL 1985

Brian Williams successfully converted two penalties as Rovers comfortably defeated Brentford 3-0 at Eastville in a Third Division fixture. In fact, Williams came within an ace of becoming the first Rovers player to complete a hat-trick of penalties, as a late spot kick claim was turned down by the referee. In front of a crowd of 4,519, Rovers' other scorer was Paul Bannon.

SATURDAY 7TH APRIL 1990

A 2-1 victory over Chester City may not sound unlikely, but this was Rovers' sixth consecutive 2-1 win in a league run stretching back over almost a calendar month. Before a crowd of 6,589, David Mehew and Christian McLean scored for the second game in succession. Oddly, Rovers had trailed at half-time in three of those six consecutive victories and, in fact, had defeated Cardiff City through two goals in injury time. At the end of the season, Rovers were Third Division champions.

TUESDAY 8TH APRIL 1958

Sandy Bay on the island of St. Vincent in the West Indies was the birthplace of Errington Edison Kelly, who scored three goals for Rovers in the 1982-83 season. A striker, Kelly was to represent Rovers in twelve (plus six as a substitute) league matches between February 1982 and his January 1983 transfer to Lincoln City. He played league football with both Bristol clubs, Lincoln City and Peterborough United before trying his luck in Sweden.

SATURDAY 9TH APRIL 1921

When Rovers drew 1-1 at home to Merthyr Town in Division Three, the visitors' equaliser was scored by Rees Williams, with a shot so hard that it broke the back of the Eastville net. Rovers had been leading through a goal from Sid Leigh until Williams' fierce shot stunned the 9,000 crowd.

MONDAY 9TH APRIL 1928

A professional with Rovers from February 1952, Paddy Hale was born in Clevedon. He scored against Leicester City on his debut, but this was one of only twelve goals in 120 league appearances for Rovers, many as a centre-half.

MONDAY 9TH APRIL 1928

Only one player has represented Rovers in the Football League past his 39th birthday and Welsh-speaking Jack Evans played his last match for Rovers in a 1-1 draw with Crystal Palace, aged 39 years 68 days. Evans, a Welsh international who had also been Cardiff City's first professional player, remains Rovers' oldest league goalscorer too, having scored his final goal for the club in a defeat at Bournemouth the previous December. Born in Bala in 1889, Jack Evans was the first Cardiff player to score a goal at Ninian Park and died in the Welsh capital in 1971.

FRIDAY 10TH APRIL 1998

Peter Beadle, who had scored a nine-minute hat-trick for Rovers some 18 months earlier, added three goals in eleven minutes to see off Wigan Athletic. His goals, after 45, 51 and 56 minutes, after Barry Hayles and Tom Ramasut had already put Rovers two goals ahead, helped Rovers to a comfortable 5-0 victory in front of a crowd of 6,038 at the Memorial Stadium. Beadle scored 39 league goals in his three years with Rovers before joining Port Vale in 1998.

SATURDAY 11TH APRIL 1891

The 5-1 defeat at Warmley, in which Archie Laurie scored a consolation goal, Rovers having trailed only 1-0 at the interval, marks the sole appearance for Rovers of Lewis Frank, a centre-forward who was born in 1862 in Russia and emigrated to Leeds as a child. He married Etty, a British national who had been born in Germany but settled in Leeds, and they had five children. By 1901, Frank was living in Bedminster and working as a tailor; his date of death remains unknown.

SATURDAY 11TH APRIL 1903

The Eastville pitch has seen many things down the years, but perhaps no sport as unusual as American Pushball. A Stapleton Road XV took on unknown opponents in front of a crowd of 3,000 who were perhaps as bemused as we are by a sport that uses a ball that was five feet six inches in height, weighing 40 pounds and costing £35. The Stapleton Road XV won 10-4.

TUESDAY 12TH APRIL 1983

Keith Curle, a teenager destined to play for England later in his career, scored the fastest goal in Rovers' Football League history and was later sent off. Rovers took the lead after just 25 seconds, but were forced to finish the match with only ten men, Dean White's second-half equaliser earning Millwall a 1-1 draw in this Third Division game played at The Den. Marcus Stewart scored after 26 seconds against Hull City in January 1996 and Marcus Bignot's goal against Bristol City in December 2000 came after 27 seconds.

MONDAY 13TH APRIL 1936

What best epitomised Rovers' inter-war struggle was the disastrous 12-0 defeat at Luton Town's Kenilworth Road in front of a crowd of 13,962. Luton, in an injury crisis, promoted reserve wing-half Joe Payne to centre-forward and he scored ten times to set a Football League record unsurpassed to this day. The minutes of Payne's goals, which included eight in a 38-minute burst and constituted three headers and seven shots, were timed as: 23, 40, 43, 49, 55, 57, 65, 76, 84 and 86. Payne went on to play for England. The other goals were scored by Fred Roberts, who netted the second of four first-half goals, and George Martin, who scored the twelfth. Not surprisingly, this grim day in Rovers' history is the heaviest defeat suffered by the club in competitive football, though supporters will also grimace at the memory of a 9-0 defeat by Spurs and 8-1 losses at both Swansea and Torquay United; the club has also conceded eight in two FA Cup-ties and once lost 7-0 at home to Grimsby Town.

FRIDAY 14TH APRIL 1911

Good Friday was not an appropriate description of the 1-0 home win against champions-elect Swindon Town in the Southern League, which Rovers gained through Jack Rankin's goal before a 15,000 crowd at Eastville. From start to finish, the match was played at a ferocious pace and the final ten minutes were characterised by a series of nasty fouls. Having been warned by referee Mr. Pellowe, the two captains, Rovers' Bill Shaw and Swindon's Charlie Bannister, were both sent off with two minutes remaining and the visitors' robust left-back Jock Walker left the field with a police escort.

THURSDAY 14TH APRIL 1949

Bruce Bannister was born in Bradford, Yorkshire. He joined Rovers in November 1971 in a £23,000 deal after six years with his home-town club and swiftly forged an exciting striking partnership with Alan Warboys, with the strikers being known nationally as "Smash and Grab". Bannister himself played in 202 (plus four as substitute) league matches for Rovers, his 80 goals including three at Brighton & Hove Albion in December 1973, when Warboys added four in an 8-2 victory. Bannister also played for Plymouth Argyle and Hull City – as well as a spell in France – before setting up a hugely successful sports shoe business in Bradford. Any list of favourite players, put together by supporters, is likely to include the names of the popular duo Warboys and Bannister.

TUESDAY 15TH APRIL 1919

The death in Bristol of Samuel Sinclair Rinder brought to an end a long personal association with Bristol Rovers. Born in South London in 1854, Rinder was the oldest of seven children to a street paving surveyor John and his wife Johanna Sutcliffe. He had played in goal for Rovers in one game in 1888, gave support to the embryonic club and, from 1897, was a club director. An ostrich feather manufacturer by profession, he lived in Stapleton Road and was married to Anne Smith, and had two sons, Charles and Austin.

SATURDAY 15TH APRIL 1922

A disastrous afternoon at Swansea ended up in defeat by the score of 8-1 against a side Rovers realistically could have hoped to beat. Steve Sims and Joe Walter both left the field injured before half-time and, with Bill Panes also a passenger, Rovers struggled in these days before substitutes. Swansea were 5-0 up by half-time and the score was only kept down by stand-in goalkeeper Jack Thomson's heroics between the sticks. Jimmy Collins scored four times, Bill Brown three and Joe Spottiswood once, with Jimmy Haydon replying for Rovers before a 3,000 crowd at the Vetch Field. Rovers' players have also scored notable hat-tricks on this day; on April 15th 1927, Bill Culley became, at 34 years 232 days, Rovers' oldest hat-trick scorer in the league, whilst David Mehew, on this day in 1988, became the youngest at 20 years 168 days.

MONDAY 15TH APRIL 1935

The Third Division (South) Cup Final was played at Millwall before a poor crowd of 2,000. The Den had been selected as a neutral venue after Rovers and Watford had refused to toss a coin to decide home advantage. On a very wet surface Rovers were a goal ahead at half-time, through Bobby McKay's 20th-minute shot. Shortly after half-time, McNestry crossed for Charlie Wipfler to score and with captain Jock McLean leading from the back, Rovers looked in control. Even when Bill Lane pulled a goal back with eight minutes remaining, Irvine Harwood put Rovers 3-1 ahead. In the dying seconds, Vic O'Brien added a second for Watford, but Rovers had won their first major honour in 30 years.

MONDAY 15TH APRIL 1968

In the days when three fixtures were played in four days, Good Friday, Easter Saturday and Easter Monday, Rovers kicked off at Torquay United's Plainmoor at the club's earliest ever kick-off time of 10.30am, in front of a healthy attendance of 11,401. Rovers had defeated Torquay at home by a single Stuart Taylor goal before losing 3-1 at Stockport County and now lost 2-0, with Trevor Shepherd scoring twice for Torquay.

SATURDAY 16TH APRIL 1921

Inside-forward Sam Baldie was born in the town of Scoon. He spent the first two post-war seasons at Eastville, when he appeared in eight league matches, scoring four goals. Formerly at Luton Town, Rovers proved to be the only club where he gained league experience. Following a fruitless trial at Crystal Palace, he spent four seasons with Chippenham Town before joining Minehead in 1952. Baldie died in Bristol in November 1998, at the age of 77.

MONDAY 17TH APRIL 1972

Barrington Edward Hayles, known universally as Barry, was born in London of Jamaican parentage. Signing for Rovers from Stevenage Borough, he scored in his first three league games and totalled 34 goals in 66 league matches between August 1997 and November 1998 and proved to be a popular and charismatic striker. Having left Rovers he played for Fulham, Sheffield United, Millwall, Plymouth Argyle, Leicester City and Cheltenham Town.

SATURDAY 18TH APRIL 1931

Fred Le May, who played in Thames' 4-0 defeat at Eastville in December 1930 and their 2-1 home defeat against Rovers, was the shortest player to play against Rovers in league football. Measuring exactly five feet tall, Frederick John Sidney Le May enjoyed a long career with three London sides, Thames, Watford and Orient. He weighed seven stone and ten pounds.

MONDAY 18TH APRIL 1949

Alan Warboys was born in Goldthorpe, Yorkshire, four days after the birth of Bruce Bannister, who was to be his colleague-in-arms as 'Smash and Grab' in Rovers' 1973-74 promotion campaign. Having played for both Sheffield clubs, Doncaster Rovers and Cardiff City, Warboys arrived at Eastville in a £35,000 deal in March 1973 with a wealth of experience. His 53 goals for Rovers in 141 (plus three as substitute) league appearances included four in the televised 8-2 victory away to Brighton in December 1973, and hat-tricks against Southport and Southend United. He later played for Fulham and Hull City before returning to Doncaster Rovers.

FRIDAY 19TH APRIL 1901

Jimmy Kedens was born in the Scottish town of Auchinleck, one of 13 children born into a mining family. An outside-left with Sherburn Rovers and Ardeer Thistle, he joined Rovers in December 1926 for £50 and made one league appearance when the veteran Jack Evans was attending his mother's funeral. Sadly for Kedens, Rovers lost 7-0 and he was released at the end of that season. Later with Glenburn Rovers for almost a decade, Kedens returned to coalmining in Scotland and died, unmarried, in Prestwick in January 1975 at the age of 73.

FRIDAY 19TH APRIL 1974

A goalless draw at Southend United gave Rovers the point they required to secure promotion to Division Two. A crowd of 8,323 at Roots Hall saw Rovers take to the field with Jim Eadie in goal, Trevor Jacobs and Lindsay Parsons at full-back, with Peter Aitken, Stuart Taylor, Frankie Prince, David Staniforth, Tom Stanton, Alan Warboys, Bruce Bannister and John Rudge comprising the team. After a long unbeaten run, the side limped across the line to promotion.

SATURDAY 20TH APRIL 1963

The circumstances surrounding Rovers' 2-2 draw at Bradford Park Avenue, when Hugh Ryden and Bobby Jones scored for Rovers before a crowd of 6,794, drew national attention. The *Sunday People* newspaper alleged that Rovers' goalkeeper Esmond Million had accepted a £300 bribe to let Rovers lose and had conceded two goals to Avenue's bright young striker Kevin Hector. Million and his accomplice, Rovers' top scorer Keith Williams, received no money and were suspended by the club pending a legal investigation. That July they were fined £50 each in court and banned from football for life. Rovers' immediate and helpful response came in for high praise.

SATURDAY 21ST APRIL 1956

The largest crowd at any Football League match involving Bristol Rovers was the 49,274 at Elland Road to see the Second Division fixture against Leeds United. Going into this game, Rovers were in second place and an automatic promotion position to the top division. Victory for Rovers would mean that only a point was required from the final game, at home to Liverpool, so the Supporters' Club chartered an aeroplane for the trip. Dai Ward set a club record by scoring for an eighth successive game, when he headed home a George Petherbridge cross after just two minutes and Rovers' hopes were raised. John Charles and Jack Overfield, though, both scored before half-time to give Leeds victory and they took the second promotion place in Rovers' stead.

THURSDAY 22ND APRIL 1937

An alert watchman at Eastville Stadium spotted and put out a fire in a storeroom beneath one of the stands. Tom Berry, who was employed by the Bristol Greyhound Company, spotted smoke coming from a store room next to the changing rooms at 11pm; by 4am, two fire engines had the situation under control, though some kit was lost in the blaze. It was widely recognised at the time that only Berry's prompt action had prevented a disaster. In August 1980, a fire was to destroy the South Stand and hasten Rovers' later departure from the old ground that the club had called its own since 1897.

SUNDAY 23RD APRIL 1922

Jim Allaway, an amateur inside-forward who played in four league matches for Brough Fletcher's Rovers in the first post-war league season, was born in Bristol. He made his debut in the first post-war season, but Rovers picked up just one point from his four outings in the first team. After a season with Rovers, he joined Bristol City in 1947 but was unable to break into the side. He subsequently played for Glastonbury, Bath City, Trowbridge Town, where he was the club's top scorer, Chippenham Town, Street and Bridgwater Town.

SATURDAY 24TH APRIL 1897

Occasionally teams are reduced to nine men through two red cards. Clifton Association, though, played the entire match against Rovers two men short – and Rovers still lost the game. Clifton arrived at Eastville with only nine players, due to transport problems, but Rovers put in "a wretched performance" (*Western Daily Press*) to lose 2-0.

SATURDAY 24TH APRIL 1993

Relegation to Division Three was confirmed as Rovers lost at West Ham United. Facing the daunting task of requiring three straight wins to retain their status, Rovers took the lead after half-time in front of a 16,682 crowd, when central defender Billy Clark struck the ball home. However, relegation duly followed as Julian Dicks (penalty) and David Speedie scored the goals to defeat Rovers 2-1.

SATURDAY 25TH APRIL 1953

In winning 3-1 at home to Newport County in front of a 29,451 crowd, Rovers secured promotion to Division Two. With impeccable timing, Geoff Bradford, having already established a new club seasonal record, scored a majestic hat-trick to send Rovers up to the heady heights of Division Two for the first time. A talisman with a golden touch, Bradford was inevitably going to have the final say in Rovers' promotion push. His first-minute side-foot was followed by headers after 40 and 70 minutes, whilst beleaguered County, who had at one stage equalised through George Beattie's shot off the underside of the crossbar, lost goalkeeper Harry Fearnley with a broken collar-bone. Bradford's season tally had reached 33, a figure never bettered, though Rickie Lambert, with his 29 league strikes in 2008-09, came close.

TUESDAY 25TH APRIL 1905

The Southern League championship was secured with a game to spare, as Brentford were defeated 3-0 at Eastville in front of an ecstatic 5,000 crowd. It was Rovers' first significant honour. Inside-left Andy Smith scored twice, one a penalty, whilst Welsh international inside-right Jack Lewis chipped in with a goal too. Undefeated at home all season, as was to be the case again in the 1989-90 Third Division championship season, Rovers finished the campaign five points clear of second-placed Reading.

SATURDAY 26TH APRIL 1986

Though no one was to know it at the time, a tepid end-of-season 1-1 draw with Chesterfield was to be Rovers' final competitive fixture at their Eastville Stadium spiritual home. Trevor Morgan for Rovers and Brian Scrimgeour for the Spireites exchanged goals in front of a crowd of 3,576. After this end-of-season encounter, the club's home was sold on and gradually dismantled. The final floodlight was taken down on December 4th 2003 and various parts of it were sold at auction ten days later.

SATURDAY 27TH APRIL 1963

Steve Williams, who became Rovers' second youngest league scorer in December 1980, aged 17 years 208 days, was born in Barry. He joined Rovers as an apprentice and made his league debut at the age of 17. That goal against Notts County, though, in a 1-1 draw at Eastville, proved to be the only one he scored in eight league appearances and he joined Barry Town in August 1982 before playing for many years in senior non-league football either side of the River Severn. He died in December 1999, aged just 36.

SATURDAY 28TH APRIL 1928

Emma Slee, a noted London dancer, was the guest of honour at Taunton Town and kicked-off the Southern League game between that club and Rovers' reserve side. A crowd of 1,500 had gathered and Rovers fielded a side that included ten players with Football League experience. Having fallen behind to a Clemmett goal ten minutes from time, Rovers reserves equalised three minutes later through Bill Culley, only to lose to inside-right Morgan's 89th-minute winner.

SATURDAY 28TH APRIL 1962

Relegation to Division Three was confirmed by Rovers' 2-0 defeat at the hands of Luton Town before a crowd of 6,555 at Kenilworth Road. Gordon Turner put the Hatters ahead after three minutes, following a poor goal-kick by Howard Radford, and Alec Ashworth's shot twelve minutes later was deflected in off Dave Bumpstead so that Rovers, in losing 2-0, were relegated with Brighton & Hove Albion to Division Three, three points adrift of Leeds United.

TUESDAY 28TH APRIL 1987

A series of waterlogged pitches had led to a fixture pile-up at the end of the 1986-87 season and Rovers were glancing nervously over their collective shoulders as relegation threatened. Victory over Chester City in front of a miserly 2,323 crowd helped Rovers considerably towards the safety they ultimately found, but the game could have evolved very differently. Ricky Greenhough and Stuart Rimmer twice gave Chester the lead before their midfielder Graham Barrow was sent off on the stroke of half-time. In the second half, Rovers stepped up a gear and won 3-2, with Jeff Meacham contributing two equalisers and John Scales, a future England defender, scoring a spectacular 25-yard winning goal after 72 minutes, arguably the best goal seen in Rovers' decade at Twerton Park.

SATURDAY 29TH APRIL 1939

A poor season ended in a catastrophic defeat at Brighton & Hove Albion in front of a 3,000 crowd. For the third of only five occasions in Rovers' history, three separate opponents scored twice each in Rovers' 6-3 defeat. Herbert Goffey, Herbert Stephens and Robert Farrell were on the mark as Rovers conceded three goals in each half. Tommy Mills scored once and Frank Curran twice, including Rovers' final inter-war league goal. He was to contribute Rovers' next league goal, too, against Reading in August 1946.

SUNDAY 29TH APRIL 2007

Strikingly blond centre-forward Ted Purdon died in Toronto at the age of 77. Originally from South Africa, Purdon had spent a decade in England with Birmingham City, Sunderland, Workington and Barrow before scoring once in only four league matches with Rovers in the 1960-61 season. He emigrated to Canada in the summer of 1961.

SATURDAY 30TH APRIL 1910

Only once in Rovers' long history has the club's goalkeeper scored. In the end-of-season game at Queens Park Rangers, with Rovers trailing by two goals, the side were awarded an 80th-minute penalty following a trip on Adam McColl. Peter Roney, the reliable goalkeeper who was to appear in 178 Southern League matches for the club, was entrusted with the penalty and he made no mistake. Rovers lost this Southern League fixture 2-1 before a crowd of 6,000 at the Park Royal Ground.

SATURDAY 30TH APRIL 1983

The last league goal ever scored by any of the eleven players that lifted the World Cup for England in 1966 was the 25-yard shot through which Alan Ball gave Rovers a single-goal victory over Huddersfield Town before a crowd of 9,819 at Eastville. Having joined Rovers in January 1983, this was the second goal Ball scored in 17 league appearances with Rovers. Once the subject of an English transfer record, Ball had earned a plethora of England caps and had featured in two decades of league football for many of the country's top clubs. He died in April 2007.

MONDAY 30TH APRIL 2001

Facing a backlog of league fixtures and requiring four points from three games to avoid relegation to the basement division for the first time in the club's history, Rovers lost 3-0 at home to Port Vale before a crowd of 3,962. Without Robbie Pethick, Che Wilson, Lewis Hogg and Christian Lee, Rovers recalled Mark McKeever, Ronnie Maugé, Ansah Owusu and Richie Partridge to the side for what was their ninth match in a calendar month. Level until 18 minutes from time, Dwayne Plummer's own goal and strikes from Marc Bridge-Wilkinson and Tony Naylor consigned Rovers to defeat and relegation followed two days later.

BRISTOL ROVERS
On This Day

MAY

TUESDAY 1st MAY 1956

Tom Brandon, who played in 26 Southern League matches for Rovers in the 1919-20 season, prior to Rovers' elevation to the Football League the following summer, died in Liverpool, at the age of 62. Born in Blackburn, his father Tom and cousin Harry Brandon played professional football, whilst his brothers Jim and Bob were on Sheffield United's books. Brandon was a strong-tackling full-back with much Football League experience. Having made his West Ham United debut at Eastville against Rovers in September 1913, Brandon later played in the league with Hull City, Bradford Park Avenue and Wigan Borough.

MONDAY 2nd MAY 1921

Exeter City were defeated 5-0 at Eastville, with Sid Leigh scoring four times. Despite the fact that Rovers have enjoyed continuous membership of the Football League since then, no Rovers player has ever scored more than four times in a league game. Not only was Leigh the first player to score so many goals in one league fixture for the club, but he also became the first player to score a first-half hat-trick for the club. Only 14 first-half hat-tricks have been recorded by Bristol Rovers players during the Football League years. Against Exeter City, before a crowd of 7,000, inside-forward Ellis Crompton scored Rovers' other goal.

WEDNESDAY 2nd MAY 1990

The local derby against Bristol City had assumed gargantuan proportions. If Rovers won to preserve their unbeaten home record, promotion to Division Two would be assured, but defeat would hand the championship to the cross-city rivals. It was certainly not a night for the faint-hearted. Devon White scored from David Mehew's cross after 25 minutes and then touched home a Carl Saunders cross to double the lead, before a late Ian Holloway penalty, following handball by Andy Llewellyn, sealed a momentous 3-0 victory which propelled Rovers back into Division Two. It was a night of high drama, before a record home crowd at Twerton Park – 9,831 – that will live long in the memory of Rovers fans across the world. Three days later, needing a victory to secure the championship title, Rovers recorded a second consecutive 3-0 victory, this time at already-relegated Blackpool, to complete a remarkable season.

WEDNESDAY 2ND MAY 2001

Just eleven years after Rovers had reached the second tier of English football, they dropped, for the first time ever, into the fourth. Defeat at home to Wycombe Wanderers rendered the final-day 4-0 hammering of Wrexham irrelevant. There was a crowd of 8,264 to see if Rovers could obtain the necessary point. Danny Senda and Dannie Bulman scored second-half goals for Wycombe to put the visitors firmly in control. Although striker Kevin Gall pulled a goal back with ten minutes remaining, Rovers' inevitable relegation was confirmed.

SATURDAY 2ND MAY 2009

Rovers completed the 2008-09 season with a home win against Hartlepool United to finish the season in eleventh place. Impressive victories over Hereford United, scoring six times at home and three away, and an unlikely 5-0 victory at Walsall, had helped give Rovers supporters a feeling that the side was going places. Moreover, Rickie Lambert had spent much of the campaign as the highest goalscorer in all four divisions. Giving a first full start to Charlie Reece, Rovers were two goals up inside four minutes for the first time in the club's history and won 4-1 before a crowd of 7,363, with Jo Kuffour, Darryl Duffy, Lambert and Aaron Lescott all scoring.

MONDAY 3RD MAY 1937

James Dargue died in Townhead in Scotland, at the age of 54. Born in Blantyre in 1882, the young Scottish outside-left joined Rovers in May 1908 from Heart of Midlothian and played for Rovers in 36 Southern League matches, scoring three goals. Formerly with Glossop North End, for whom he appeared in seven Second Division games in 1905-06, he played for Airdrie and Hearts. In September 1909 he signed for Royal Albert and also played for Hamilton Academicals in the 1913-14 season.

SATURDAY 4TH MAY 1912

In a match to raise money for the Titanic Disaster Fund, Rovers lost 3-1 to Bristol City before a crowd of 1,500. Bill Hurley gave Rovers the lead five minutes before half-time, only for City to reply with three second-half goals, the third coming from the England international centre-half Billy Wedlock.

WEDNESDAY 4TH MAY 1960

"Socby" never caught on as a sport, but this game of football with a rugby ball was played at the Memorial Ground, as it was then known, with Rovers in quarters defeating Bristol Rugby Club in all-yellow 3-1, after second-half goals from Geoff Bradford (two), Peter Hooper and the rugby club captain John Blake. £450 was raised for the Friends of Frenchay Hospital, whose chairman at this time was the Rovers manager, Bert Tann.

SATURDAY 5TH MAY 1923

It would appear that the only goal Rovers have scored direct from a corner was the one scored by Tosh Parker to give Rovers a 1-0 victory at Swansea in a Third Division (South) encounter. The fact that no other player touched the ball indicates that this goal should, in fact, have been disallowed, as the law allowing goals to be scored from corners did not appear until June 1924. Nonetheless, the goal was allowed to stand; the referee, H. C. Curtis, had failed to show up for the game, which was refereed by linesman U. Jones of Ton Pentre.

TUESDAY 5TH MAY 1959

Rovers took a sensational lead in the Gloucestershire Cup Final before an Eastville crowd of 11,022, with the fastest goal ever recorded in the club's history. Sweeping forward from the kick-off, Dai Ward scored after only seven seconds, but Bert Tindill's second-half equaliser for Bristol City left the score all square.

SATURDAY 5TH MAY 1990

Rovers had secured promotion to Division Two in their penultimate game of the season. Yet, to ensure that local rivals Bristol City could not steal the championship away, victory was essential at already-relegated Blackpool in the final game. Over 5,000 Rovers supporters made the trip to Bloomfield Road in a crowd of 6,776, where a second successive 3-0 victory, with Phil Purnell scoring in the final minute of the first half, to add to David Mehew's earlier goal, and substitute Paul Nixon's in the 90th minute, saw Rovers secure the championship in a carnival atmosphere. Vaughan Jones was able to lift the trophy at his own testimonial game a week later.

MONDAY 6TH MAY 1968

Ian Weston, the first Rovers player to be sent off on his club debut, was born in Bristol. Aged just 18, Weston was shown a red card after 50 minutes of a 2-0 FA Cup defeat at Brentford in December 1986 before making his league debut. He was to play for Rovers in 13 (plus there as substitute) league matches without scoring, as a defensive midfielder, before spending two seasons with Torquay United and playing for the Gulls at Wembley. Thereafter he played for several local non-league sides including Bath City, Cheltenham Town, Weston-super-Mare and Clevedon Town.

SATURDAY 7TH MAY 1927

On four occasions Rovers were the winners of the Allen Palmer Cup, a tournament established in 1924 by Brigadier-General George Llewellyn Palmer, a former MP for Westbury, Wiltshire, and his wife Louie Madeleine (née Gouldsmith) in memory of their son, who had been killed during World War I. Joe Clennell's goal brought about a 1-0 victory over Bristol City and Rovers were to win the tournament on three further occasions, defeating Nottingham Forest in 1933, Southampton in 1935 and Bournemouth, after extra time, twelve months later.

THURSDAY 7TH MAY 1959

Tony Sealy, who was to appear in 21 (plus 16 as substitute) league matches for Rovers, scoring on seven occasions, was born in Hackney. He held the astonishing record of having won four championship medals with four different clubs in the space of a decade in a career that also took him to Sporting Lisbon and a Wembley appearance in the 1979 League Cup Final.

SATURDAY 7TH MAY 2005

The shortest league career of any Rovers player is precisely one minute. That was the time spent on the field by Rovers substitute Louie Soares against Wycombe Wanderers; he never played for Rovers again. Twenty-year-old midfielder Soares was on loan to Rovers from Reading, for whom he never played, but later tasted Football League action with Barnet and Aldershot Town. In January 2007 he won a first cap for Barbados against Trinidad and Tobago, whilst his brother Tom has made his name at Crystal Palace.

MONDAY 8TH MAY 1899

Jack Leonard, a 21-year-old Bristolian inside-forward, who was to play for Rovers in five Southern League matches, scoring twice, joined the club from local rivals Bedminster. He had played in 24 Southern League games, scoring seven goals prior to his arrival at Eastville and was to join Small Heath, now Birmingham City, where he played in seven Second Division games, scoring once, before ending his career at Cheltenham Town. Jack Leonard died in the spring of 1917 in Bristol.

FRIDAY 8TH MAY 1931

Joe Calvert, a coalminer from Frickley Colliery, joined Rovers, where he was to remain for a season. Twenty-four years old and over six feet tall, Calvert was an ever-present in his season at Eastville which included an 8-1 defeat at Torquay United. After 42 league appearances in goal, he moved to Leicester City, where he played in 72 league matches between 1932 and 1948. Leicester's oldest ever player – past his 40th birthday – he also became the second oldest ever player at Watford, making five league appearances in the spring of 1948. Calvert died in Leicester in December 1999, aged 92.

TUESDAY 9TH MAY 1972

Penalty shoot-outs are commonplace nowadays, but the first involving Rovers came at the end of the Gloucestershire Cup Final with Bristol City at Ashton Gate, after the sides had drawn 1-1. Before a crowd of 13,137, Sandy Allan had scored Rovers' goal, with John Emanuel scoring for City. Rovers won the shoot-out 4-2. Up to the summer of 2009, Rovers had been involved in 19 penalty shoot-outs in a variety of competitions, winning 14 and losing only five.

SATURDAY 9TH MAY 1987

Only 3,160 hardy spectators were at Somerton Park, where Rovers required a point from their final-day fixture away to Newport County to avoid unprecedented relegation to Division Four. The mission was accomplished with a 1-0 win. Flying winger Phil Purnell's low shot banished any lurking fears in Rovers' supporters' minds as the game drew to a close. Rovers had spent many months hovering perilously close to the widening chasm, but lived to fight another day.

THURSDAY 10TH MAY 1906

Outside-forward Willie Gould, who was to score once in 38 Southern League appearances for Rovers, signed for the club from Second Division side Leicester Fosse. Born in 1887 in Burton-upon-Trent, Gould was the second of seven children to a brewer's labourer and escaped the beer trade through his football. He played in the Football League for Burton United and Leicester before his spell at Eastville and, having left Rovers in May 1907 – for Glossop North End, Bradford City and Manchester City thereafter – joined Lancashire Combination side Tranmere Rovers in 1911.

WEDNESDAY 11TH MAY 1881

The celebrated England cricketer W. G. Grace moved into 57 Stapleton Road, where he set up his surgery as a General Practitioner. Not only a close neighbour of the embryonic Rovers side, Grace also refereed a number of Rovers' fixtures down the years. He had been a founder member of Stapleton Cricket Club in 1886 and represented Gloucestershire and England for many years, as the leading batsman of his generation. A huge, bearded gentleman, Grace scored the first century by an Englishman in Test cricket in the match against Australia in 1880.

WEDNESDAY 11TH MAY 1904

Hailing from a celebrated sporting family, Jack Havelock was born in Hartlepool. Signed from Army football, he was to contribute eleven goals in 20 league appearances for Rovers between 1933 and 1935. He died in Scunthorpe in July 1981. His brother Harry played for several top football clubs and their father Harold won three England caps at rugby union in 1908, the second in a 28-18 defeat to Wales at Ashton Gate in the only full rugby international ever to be staged in Bristol.

SATURDAY 11TH MAY 1946

Following the Burnden Park tragedy, in which 33 people had died, Rovers played Bristol City in a charity game to raise money for the Bolton Disaster Fund. A crowd of 9,859 saw Rovers concede six second-half goals. Don Clark scored twice for a rampant City side, with Roy Bentley, Jack Hargreaves, Cliff Morgan, Bill Thomas and Cyril Williams scoring once apiece; inside-right Sam Baldie added Rovers' consolation goal.

SATURDAY 12TH MAY 1945

Alan Ball, the only player to win a World Cup winner's medal and represent Rovers in league football, was born at his grandparents' house in Farnworth, Lancashire. A British transfer record holder in 1971, when he joined Arsenal from Everton for £220,000, Ball had started his career at Blackpool and also played for Southampton. Distinctive for his shock of red hair, his five-foot-six-inch frame and squeaky voice, Ball was the midfield dynamo that helped defeat West Germany 4-2 in the 1966 World Cup Final at Wembley and he went on to win 72 caps, scoring eight times, for his country. He joined Rovers in January 1983 and scored twice in 17 league matches before managing Portsmouth, Stoke City, Exeter City and Southampton. He died in Warsash in Hampshire in April 2007 at the age of 61.

SATURDAY 13TH MAY 1972

Peter Clifford William James Beadle, whose two goals sensationally defeated Bristol City at Ashton Gate in January 1996, was born in Lambeth. He moved to Rovers for a fee that became £50,000 in 1995, having played for Gillingham, Spurs, AFC Bournemouth, Southend United and Watford and added 39 goals for Rovers in 98 (plus eleven as substitute) league matches, which included a first-half hat-trick against Bury in November 1996, and a dramatic last-minute equaliser at Ashton Gate two weeks later. He later played for Port Vale, Notts County, Bristol City, Brentford and Barnet before managing Taunton Town and Newport County.

TUESDAY 13TH APRIL 1974

Inside-forward Charles Heinemann, born in Stafford in February 1904, died in Hornchurch at the age of 70. The first three matches of 1925-26 proved to be his only league appearances, though he enjoyed many seasons with Stafford Rangers and Oakengates Town.

SUNDAY 14TH MAY 1933

AC Milan defeated Rovers 3-1 in a match played at the Stade St. Maurice in Nice. George McNestry scored Rovers' goal from the penalty spot early in the second half, with Rovers already two goals behind. Romani scored twice for Milan. Four days later, McNestry was again on the score-sheet as Rovers lost 3-1 to a French XI.

SATURDAY 15TH MAY 1965

John Graham, a Rovers forward in the 1902-03 season, died in Saltcoats, at the age of 83. Born in the Ayrshire town of Dalry in August 1881, he signed for Rovers from Kilmarnock in May 1902, having scored 14 goals in 37 Scottish League games at Rugby Park, and appeared in 17 Southern League matches, scoring four times. In May 1903 he left Rovers to join Celtic before moving to Millwall in 1904 and Accrington a year later. He had represented the Scottish League against the Irish League in 1901.

WEDNESDAY 15TH MAY 1974

Rovers' tour of Australia took in a fixture against a Coalfields XI that comprised players from Newcastle, Cessnock and Maitland. The match attracted a crowd of 6,000 to Weston Park, Weston, New South Wales. With Stuart Taylor in dominant form at the heart of the defence, Rovers were rarely troubled and ran out comfortable 9-1 winners. Alan Warboys, David Staniforth, Bruce Bannister and John Rudge scored twice each and there was an own goal by Coalfields' Tom Sneddon.

TUESDAY 15TH MAY 1979

Welsh international Tommy Mills, who had been born in Ton Pentre in December 1911, died in Bristol at the age of 67. An inside-forward previously with Leicester City and Orient and holder of four full caps, Mills joined Rovers in April 1936 and, up to the outbreak of World War II, played in exactly 99 league games for the club, scoring 17 times.

FRIDAY 16TH MAY 1902

Jimmy Howie, one of two brothers who had played together in the Kilmarnock side, signed for Rovers from fellow Southern League side Kettering Town. An inside-forward, he scored ten goals in 26 Southern League matches with Rovers before his career took off. At Newcastle United between 1903 and 1910 he won three league championship medals and played in four FA Cup finals, as well as earning three full Scottish caps, before playing for Huddersfield Town and managing Queens Park Rangers and Middlesbrough. Born in the Ayrshire town of Galston in March 1878, Howie died in London shortly before Christmas 1962, aged 84.

SUNDAY 17TH MAY 1953

Ellis Crompton, an inside-forward who had the distinction of scoring the first goal recorded by Rovers in the Football League, died in Barnstaple at the age of 66. Born in Ramsbottom in July 1886, Crompton played league football with Blackburn Rovers and Spurs and then spent a season as Exeter City captain before signing for Rovers in May 1913 for £400. After 108 Southern League matches and 26 goals at Eastville, he added ten goals in 41 Football League matches in 1920-21 before returning to Exeter City. He later coached at Barnstaple Town, Llanelli and Barry Town. Crompton later became a publican in Barnstaple.

FRIDAY 17TH MAY 1968

After much consultation work involving Freeman, Fox and Partners, the M32 motorway was to be constructed to link the city centre with the conveniently close interchange of the north-south M5 with the M4 to London and South Wales. Work started on a 2¾-mile stretch from Muller Road to Hambrook at a cost of some £3,263,000. This new 105-foot-wide 'Parkway' superhighway, announced at a cost of £15,000,000 by city engineer James Bennett in April 1964, had led to the demolition of 200 houses. This development finally obliterated the remains of the Baptist Mills Brass Works, a major feature of the area following its inception in 1702 by the Quakers on the site of an old grist mill. A Stapleton merchant, Nehemiah Champion, had been a founder but, abandoned in 1814, all traces now lie forever hidden beneath Junction 3 of the M32. The final buildings and a pear tree appertaining to the Baptist Mills Pottery, a source of great employment in 19th-century Eastville, also vanished for eternity beneath the new construction. Few people appreciate the critical role that the building of the new motorway had on Rovers' development. Hemmed in by infrastructure, the club was unable to expand, being increasingly overlooked by a road that enabled vehicles to suffer all manner of undiagnosed ailments on its hard shoulder at around three o'clock each Saturday. Moreover, the social implications for East Bristol were immense, as cheap housing was sold off, immigrants were promised facilities that did not materialise and a greater sense of poverty pervaded the area.

SATURDAY 18TH MAY 1963

A miserly crowd of 2,126 at Halifax Town saw Rovers win a critical match with respect to the club's future. Relegation to Division Three in 1962 could have been followed by a further drop, for the first time, to the basement division. This prospect was avoided by a 3-2 win at The Shay, where 500 relieved Rovers supporters saw Bobby Jones fire Rovers ahead after just two minutes and Ian Hamilton head home Geoff Bradford's cross ten minutes later. After half-time, Halifax equalised through Paddy Stanley and Dennis Fidler, before Hamilton headed home Jones' deep cross 14 minutes from time.

THURSDAY 19TH MAY 1960

Bill Tout died in Bath, at the age of 75. Born in late 1884 in Hereford, William Edwin Brown Tout was a wing-half who played in two Southern League games for Rovers as a teenager before embarking on a long career. He spent many years first with Bristol East and later at Bath City, as well as representing the Southern League on one occasion. Later in his career he helped Swindon Town to two FA Cup semi-finals. As late as 1920, when Swindon entered the Football League, he was able to make four Third Division appearances for the Robins.

SUNDAY 20TH MAY 1990

There were some 32,000 (Bristol) Rovers fans at Wembley in the 53,317 crowd for the Leyland DAF Cup Final and, despite the result, Rovers' first game beneath the Twin Towers – against their Rovers counterparts from the Wirral – proved to be a wonderful day of celebration. A veterans' warm-up game saw Rovers and Tranmere draw 1-1, Alan Warboys and Frank Worthington scoring the goals in a show which also featured George Best and Bobby Moore OBE, and which was refereed by the veteran Jack Taylor. Just ten minutes into the final, the former Rovers defender Mark Hughes crossed and, from Chris Malkin's flick-on, Ian Muir scored. Six minutes after half-time, substitute Paul Nixon's cross found Devon White who, at the second attempt, shot right-footed high into the net for Rovers' equaliser. However, 17 minutes from time, Jim Steel's header consigned the Rovers from Bristol to a 2-1 defeat.

DEVON WHITE SCORES AT WEMBLEY IN MAY 1990

TUESDAY 20TH MAY 1997

In splashing out £150,000 to Woking for central defender Steve Foster and £200,000 to Stevenage Borough for Barry Hayles, manager Ian Holloway was beginning to piece together the side that he felt could return the glory years to Rovers. Newly returned to Bristol, the club was slowly moving forward, it was felt. Foster was to play in 193 league games (plus four as substitute), scoring seven goals over five seasons, whilst Hayles' 18 months with Rovers brought 32 goals in 62 league appearances.

SUNDAY 21ST MAY 1967

Many players have played in just one league match for Rovers down the years, one of whom Richard Iles was born in Bristol. His was the April 1986 fixture against Blackpool at Eastville where, in front of a crowd of 3,472, Rovers won through a solitary Gary Penrice strike. Iles had played for Longwell Green prior to Rovers and, released in 1986, he went on to play locally for many years, including a handful of appearances for Bath City in 1989. He once scored six goals in a match for Longwell Green Abbotonians and later worked for the Fire Brigade.

WEDNESDAY 22ND MAY 1872

Jack McLean, who played for Rovers in the 1902-03 season as a wing-half, was born in Port Glasgow. He was "a splendid footballer, a hard worker and a fearless tackler", as the Grimsby press described him at the time. Five-feet-six-inches in height, his distinguished career included junior international football for Scotland, three seasons with Liverpool and league experience with Grimsby Town and Bristol City. Signing for Rovers in May 1902, he scored once in 29 Southern League matches for before joining Millwall the following summer and he played for Queens Park Rangers for two years from 1906.

MONDAY 22ND MAY 1953

Mike Barry, a midfielder with a Welsh under-21 cap to his name, was born in Hull. Formerly at Huddersfield Town and Carlisle United, he joined Rovers in September 1977 in an exchange deal involving Jim Hamilton and added three goals in 46 (plus one as substitute) league appearances, before trying his luck in America.

TUESDAY 23RD MAY 1899

Tom Williams, who scored hat-tricks for Gillingham, Rovers, Norwich and Merthyr, was born in Ryhope, near Sunderland. Having played for Orient, Charlton Athletic, Gillingham and Ashington, he possessed a wealth of league experience prior to his arrival at Eastville in January 1926. In 75 league matches for Rovers, he scored 27 goals, which included all three as Rovers won 3-2 at Millwall in October 1926. Williams, whose brother Owen played for Orient and England, later played for Bristol City, Norwich City and Merthyr Town and died in Easington, County Durham in December 1960.

FRIDAY 23RD MAY 1975

Craig Armstrong, who appeared 13 (plus once more as substitute) times for Rovers in league action, was born in South Shields. A long career as a full-back has taken him to ten league clubs, starting as a professional at Nottingham Forest in 1992 and playing for Cheltenham Town against Rovers in September 2008, the latest of many games against the Pirates.

WEDNESDAY 24TH MAY 1995

Joe Walter's death at the age of 99 ended the life of the longest-living former Rovers player. Born in Bristol in August 1895, Walter had scored twelve goals in 89 league games for Rovers between 1920 and 1922 and again in 1928-29, as well as enjoying First Division football with both Huddersfield Town and Blackburn Rovers. The only player who opposed Rovers in league action and lived to be a hundred was Zach March, who played twice for Brighton & Hove Albion against Rovers in December 1921.

TUESDAY 25TH MAY 1937

Billy Richards, who had won a Welsh cap when he played against Northern Ireland in December 1932, joined Rovers on a free transfer from Brighton. Almost 32 and with a wealth of experience with Merthyr Town, Wolves, Coventry City, Fulham and Brighton, Richards was a quick outside-right who brought width to the Rovers side. He was, though, to play in just four Third Division (South) fixtures with Rovers before signing for Southern League Folkestone in August 1938. Billy Richards, whose brother Dai played for Wales on 21 occasions, died in Wolverhampton in September 1956, aged 51.

FRIDAY 26TH MAY 946

Regicide occurs rarely near Rovers' ground, but Edmund I, King of England since Athelstan's death in October 939, was killed in Pucklechurch, Bristol, whilst celebrating the Feast of St. Augustine. Leofa, a thief who had been thrown out of the banquet-hall, returned to the feast; the King attacked him and both men were killed in the ensuing brawl, Leofa's body being cut up into small pieces. Edmund was, at that time, married to his second wife Aethelflaed of Damerham and, in the confusing world of medieval monarchy, was succeeded to the throne by his younger brother Edred.

SUNDAY 26TH MAY 1968

For many decades they had dominated the view from Rovers' Eastville Stadium, but the famous Thirteen Arches railway bridge had been condemned and had to be demolished. 3,200 holes were drilled and when site supervisor John Turner pulled the plunger at the delayed time of 4.20pm, 6,000 spectators saw the viaduct collapse in ten seconds. It took 40 lorries to clear up 4,500 tons of masonry and brickwork. In fact, only eleven arches fell at the first attempt and one shortly afterwards; the stubborn 13th pier was blown up at 7.00am on 13th June.

SATURDAY 26TH MAY 2007

There were some 40,000 Rovers fans at Wembley in a total attendance of 61,589, the second highest crowd at any game featuring Rovers; if Rovers defeated Shrewsbury Town in the play-off final, they would have completed a remarkable end-of-season run to escape from the basement division into which the club had fallen in 2001. Yet, three minutes in, the Shrews took the lead through Stewart Drummond. Undeterred, Rovers pushed ahead through two left-footed goals from Richard Walker before half-time and, after the dismissal of Marc Tierney, a very late breakaway goal from Sammy Igoe sealed a momentous victory and long-awaited promotion before an ecstatic Rovers following. As strains of Goodnight Irene echoed around the famous stadium, Rovers could reflect on an extraordinary season that had taken the club from the potential of relegation to a place in league One as well as games at both Wembley and Cardiff's Millennium Stadium. Paul Trollope's rising reputation as one of the brightest young managers was given further impetus.

FRIDAY 27th MAY 1921

Ben Hall resigned as Rovers' manager, after Rovers had finished tenth in Division Three in their first-ever Football League season. His side had won 18 of the 42 league matches played during his stint in charge. Born in Ecclesfield, near Sheffield in 1879, Hall had played for Grimsby Town, Derby County and Leicester Fosse as a centre-half, before becoming trainer at Huddersfield Town. When Rovers were elected to the league in 1920, chairman George Humphreys appointed Hall as manager so that Alf Homer could focus on running the club's administration. After 1921, Hall scouted for Third Division (South) side Southend United. He died in 1963, aged 84.

SUNDAY 28th MAY 1995

Before a crowd of 59,175, a figure narrowly less than that for the FA Cup-tie at Newcastle in February 1951, the club made its second Wembley appearance in over one hundred years of history, for a play-off final against Huddersfield Town. Rovers had drawn twice with Crewe Alexandra in a tense play-off semi-final, only Paul Miller's scrambled equaliser at Gresty Road ensuring that the Pirates progressed to Wembley on the away-goals rule. The winner at Wembley was guaranteed promotion to the second tier of English football. Behind to an Andy Booth goal, Marcus Stewart's equaliser just seconds before half-time offered Rovers renewed hope. Stewart also hit the bar with a 35-yard shot and full-back Andy Gurney bizarrely hit his own crossbar while Gareth Taylor missed an open goal, but it was Chris Billy's diving header which brought Huddersfield Town victory and promotion.

TUESDAY 29th MAY 1900

Alec Donald, who played for Rovers in 136 league games as a reliable and strong full-back between 1932 and 1936, was born in Kirkintilloch, the second child to coalminer James Donald and his wife Jessie. Having played Scottish League football with Partick Thistle and Hearts as well as football in America with Indiana Flooring and New York Nationals, Donald brought experience to Rovers' back-line and was part of the side that secured the Third Division (South) Cup in April 1935. Having lost his place in the side to Jack Preece, Donald joined Scottish First Division side Dunfermline Athletic for a season in 1936 before coaching local sides in Scotland.

SATURDAY 30TH MAY 1964

Neil Slatter, who was the first player to win as many as ten full international caps whilst on Rovers' books, was born in Cardiff. A left-back who made his Rovers debut at the age of 16, Slatter was a key figure in the Rovers defence from 1981 to 1985, playing in 147 (plus one as substitute) league matches and scoring four times. Later with Oxford United and Bournemouth, Slatter won a total of 22 caps for Wales, but his career was cut short by a recurrent back injury and he returned to South Wales.

FRIDAY 31ST MAY 1907

A centre-back who played 13 times for Rovers in the 1935-36 season, Allan Murray was born in the Lancashire town of Heywood. Having scored once in twelve league games for Rochdale, he was to play in just one game with Fulham before signing for Rovers in May 1935. The brother-in-law of the Lancashire cricketer Frank Watson, Murray played in Rovers' 12-0 defeat at Luton Town over Easter 1936. This was hardly a new experience for him, as he had been in the Darwen side that lost 11-1 to Arsenal in the FA Cup in January 1932. He left Rovers in August 1938 to join Bath City and died in Rochdale in January 1995 at the age of 87.

THURSDAY 31ST MAY 1917

Frank Curran, who scored Rovers' last league goal before World War II and the first one thereafter, was born in Ryton-on-Tyne. Having played for Southport and Accrington Stanley in league football, Curran arrived at Eastville in June 1938 with a reputation for scoring consistently. One of three brothers to play professionally, he scored four times against Swindon Town in March 1939 to become only the fourth Rovers player to have scored that many in one league match. Curran scored 24 goals in 37 league matches for Rovers, either side of the war, and later played in Division Three (North) for Tranmere Rovers. He died in September 1998 in Southport, at the age of 81.

BRISTOL ROVERS
On This Day

JUNE

WEDNESDAY 1st JUNE 1983

Charlie Wipfler died in Petts Wood, Kent at the age of 67. Born in Trowbridge in July 1915, he had scored five times in 18 league games for Rovers as a teenager before enjoying a career with Hearts and Watford either side of World War II. He had scored one of the goals which helped Rovers defeat Watford in the 1935 Third Division (South) Cup final. He then made his Watford debut, following a £420 transfer, against Rovers on the opening day of the 1937-38 season.

TUESDAY 2nd JUNE 1964

Mark Everton Walters, who had, despite his middle name, enjoyed a long career with Liverpool, was born in Birmingham. One England cap, three Scottish League championships and two Scottish League Cup wins, both times scoring in the final, are amongst the honours accrued in a 20-year career of over 500 matches with Aston Villa, Rangers, Liverpool, Stoke City, Wolves, Southampton, Swindon Town and finally Rovers from November 1999 to April 2002. He played 46 (plus 36 as substitute) league matches for Rovers, scoring 13 goals, before enjoying many years in non-league football in the Midlands. His nephew Simon Ford was with Kilmarnock in 2009.

SATURDAY 3rd JUNE 1922

Sanger's Circus put on two shows on the pitch at Eastville. The company, then 99 years old, performed first at 2.30pm and then again at 8pm. Previously, one Rovers player had also performed in the circus; Jack Kifford, who played for Rovers in 1900-01, retired from football in 1909 to join Fred Karno's Troupe. Billy Wragg, who played for Watford against Rovers in September 1901, was also a member of Karno's and performed at the London Palladium in 1910 alongside Charlie Chaplin and Stan Laurel.

SATURDAY 3rd JUNE 1972

An experienced winger with Sheffield Wednesday, Huddersfield Town and Brighton & Hove Albion, Colin Dobson signed for Rovers as player-coach. A player whose skill excited the crowd, he was to play in 62 league matches for Rovers between 1972 and 1976, scoring four goals, before coaching at Coventry City, Port Vale and Aston Villa and trying his luck coaching football in Bahrain.

SATURDAY 4TH JUNE 1932

Bill Bann, a 29-year-old left-back, joined Rovers on a free transfer from Brentford. Born in Broxburn in August 1902, he had previously played in twelve league games for Spurs and seven for Brentford, his debut for the Bees coming against Rovers in September 1930, when he had marked Joe Pointon out of the game. Bann was to play in just one league match for Rovers, a 2-2 draw with Newport County in November 1932, though he managed seven league appearances for Aldershot in the 1933-34 season. He died in Haringey in March 1973.

MONDAY 5TH JUNE 1893

Joe Kissock was born in Coatbridge. Formerly with Vale of Clyde and having played for Bury in six Second Division games, Kissock arrived at Eastville in June 1921 and broke into Rovers' side after regular left-back Jack Stockley broke his leg. He was to represent Rovers in 18 Third Division (South) fixtures in the 1921-22 season before returning north of the border that summer to join Peebles Rovers. A few months in the USA preceded a move to New Zealand in May 1923. Kissock so impressed for Hospital AFC that he won 15 full caps for New Zealand, scoring once on his international debut. He later moved back to the States and died in San Francisco in September 1959, aged 66.

SATURDAY 6TH JUNE 1900

The third son of Richard, a coalminer originally from North Wales, Richard Jones was born in Ashton-in-Makerfield. Formerly with Oldham Athletic, Rochdale and Stockport County, Jones joined Rovers from Exeter City in June 1925 and played wing-half in eight league fixtures before moving on to Colwyn Bay United and later Northwich Victoria.

WEDNESDAY 6TH JUNE 1973

The only player who has appeared for Rovers as well as being sent off playing for his country was Alan Ball. The flame-haired, combative Arsenal midfielder was given his marching orders whilst playing for England against Poland in a World Cup qualifying game in Chorzow that finished goalless. Ball joined Rovers in January 1983 and scored twice in 17 league appearances whilst at Eastville.

SATURDAY 7TH JUNE 1975

Jack Smith, who played four times for Rovers as a full-back in the 1934-35 season died in Weymouth at the age of 63. Born in Merthyr Tydfil in the autumn of 1911, Arthur John Smith trained first as a dentist, but gave this up to play league football for Wolves. He then joined Rovers before moving to Swindon Town, Chelsea and West Bromwich Albion, in wartime football. His career ended in bizarre circumstances, as his foot was run over by a bus during a wartime blackout. Later a coach at Wolves and manager at both Reading and West Bromwich Albion, he retired in 1955 to run a public house in Weymouth.

TUESDAY 8TH JUNE 1897

Jack Jones joined Rovers from Small Heath, the modern-day Birmingham City. Over the next few years, he was to score 49 goals in 61 Birmingham and District League games and 36 in 76 Southern League matches, after Rovers' elevation to that league in 1899. He added a club record six goals in the 15-1 FA Cup win against Weymouth in 1900 and five more against the same opposition a year later. The 1901 census shows Jack Jones and his wife Jane living in Park Crescent, Eastville with their first child, Archibald. Born in West Bromwich in October 1874, Jones signed for Spurs in May 1902 but died of typhoid in Edmonton the following year, aged just 26, leaving a pregnant widow and two young sons. When his widow remarried, to a milkman called Fletcher, the three sons took their stepfather's name and, in time, acquired two half-sisters. The whole family soon emigrated to the United States.

SATURDAY 9TH JUNE 1900

Jack Price, who played five times for Rovers as a left-back during the 1923-24 season was born in Ibstock, Leicestershire. Previously on the books of Leicester City with his brother Fred and their uncle Cliff, 'Ginger' Price later played league football for both Swindon Town and Torquay United and later coached football and cricket at Charterhouse School. By 1929 he was running a greengrocer's shop in Torquay. He later moved back to Leicestershire and died in Coalville in November 1984, aged 84.

SATURDAY 10TH JUNE 1961

Nicky Platnauer, who scored seven goals for Rovers in 21 (plus three as substitute) league matches in the 1982-83 season, was born in Leicester. A blond-haired attacking full-back who also played on occasions in attack, Platnauer had been recommended to Rovers' manager Bobby Gould by his brother Trevor, who was in charge of Bedford Town and he was signed in July 1982. He later played league football for ten other clubs, before managing a string of sides in the East Midlands.

SUNDAY 11TH JUNE 1967

Wayne Noble, an England Youth squad player who appeared for Rovers in 16 (plus five as substitute) league matches, scoring once, between 1985 and 1987, was born in Bristol. A teenage midfielder throughout his time at Eastville, Noble scored in a 2-2 draw with Newport County at Eastville in December 1986 and later played locally for many sides, including Yeovil Town, Gloucester City and Bath City. He has worked as a travel agent, a publican and a delivery driver, as well as helping Rovers as a Football in the Community coach since 2004.

SATURDAY 12TH JUNE 1880

Arthur Cartlidge, a long-serving Rovers goalkeeper, was born. A 1901 signing from Stoke, his home-town club, Cartlidge represented Rovers in 258 Southern League games and won a Southern League championship medal in 1904-05, before joining top-flight side Aston Villa in April 1909. Having won a league championship medal at Villa, he rejoined Stoke in 1911. He died in Stoke in May 1922, aged 41.

FRIDAY 12TH JUNE 1925

Having played five times for Charlton Athletic, centre-half Alf Bowers joined Rovers ahead of the 1925-26 season. He was to play in three league matches for Rovers and in one for Queens Park Rangers, a club he joined in August 1926. Rovers lost home and away to Exeter City with Bowers in the side and recorded a 2-0 victory at home to Gillingham. Born at home in Bethnal Green in April 1895, Alf Bowers was the fourth child of a vellum binder in the print industry, John Bowers, and his wife Alice Fowler.

FRIDAY 12TH JUNE 1936

Don Megson, who represented Rovers both as a player and as a manager, was born in the Cheshire town of Sale. A full-back, who had played for Sheffield Wednesday in 386 league games, scoring six times, as well as captaining the Owls to the 1966 FA Cup final, Megson signed for Rovers in March 1970 as player-coach. He was to play in 31 league matches with Rovers, scoring once, before becoming the fourth former Wednesday player to manage Rovers. Between 1972 and 1977, when he took over at Portland Timbers in North America, he led Rovers to a Watney Cup triumph and promotion to Division Two. His elder son Gary Megson played in 499 league matches for a range of teams, before managing eight league clubs, including West Bromwich Albion and Bolton Wanderers in the top flight.

THURSDAY 13TH JUNE 1996

Ian Holloway, already a legendary figure in Rovers circles, became manager of the club; he was to remain in the post until January 2001. The third child to local footballer Bill Holloway and his wife Jean, Ian was born in March 1963 in Bristol. Holloway had made his mark as an enthusiastic teenage midfielder who developed into an essential cog in a Rovers side that ultimately won the Third Division championship in 1989-90. Despite spells away at Wimbledon, Brentford, Torquay United and Queens Park Rangers, he was to play in 379 (plus 18 as substitute) league matches for Rovers, scoring 42 goals between 1981 and 1999. An essential ingredient in the Rovers story, Holloway later managed QPR, Plymouth Argyle and Leicester City.

SATURDAY 14TH JUNE 1969

Richard Dryden, who played both as a winger and as a full-back at Rovers, was born in Stroud. Having played in twelve (plus one as substitute) league matches in his time at Eastville, he joined Exeter City in March 1989 in a £10,000 deal and later played for several other clubs as a resolute and dependable central defender. In his first season at St. James' Park, Exeter were crowned Fourth Division champions. He totalled eleven league clubs in his career, before spending time in the Conference with Scarborough and became manager at Worcester City in November 2007.

FUTURE ROVERS PLAYER AND MANAGER DON MEGSON WAS BORN IN JUNE 1936

WEDNESDAY 15TH JUNE 1898

Dick Allan, an inside-forward who played in four Birmingham and District League games for Rovers in the 1898-99 season, joined Bristol St. George from Newcastle United. Born in Preston in the autumn of 1877, he had appeared for his home-town club and Newcastle in the Football League, as well as for Dundee. A brief spell at Bristol St. George preceded an even shorter period at Eastville, though he scored against Hereford Thistle in April 1899. Now converted to left-back, Allan joined Stockport County in the summer of 1903 and played 22 times in the league in 1903-04. The son of Preston plumber Henry and his wife Mary, Dick Allan died in Prestwich, Lancashire in 1923.

THURSDAY 16TH JUNE 1927

Jack Thom, an inside-forward who scored four goals in his six Third Division (South) appearances for Rovers in the 1927-28 season, joined Rovers in a deal worth £175. Born in the Ayrshire town of Hurlford, Thom was previously on the books of Nottingham Forest. He had made his league bow with Leeds United, from whom Rovers secured his services. After a successful two years with Workington, which included 69 goals in the 1928-29 season, he added almost one hundred goals for Aldershot, before playing for Guildford City and Basingstoke Town. He died in Aldershot in August 1966 at the age of 67.

SUNDAY 17TH JUNE 1979

Sir Hubert Ashton, who played in one league game for Rovers, died in South Weald aged 81. Born in Calcutta in 1898, the fourth son of a prominent Victorian businessman, Ashton played in the 4-1 defeat at Reading in May 1925, Hugh Davey scoring a hat-trick, and also represented Orient in league action. A Cambridge blue at cricket, football and hockey, Ashton was a Conservative MP from 1950 to 1964, High Sheriff of Essex in 1943 and President of the MCC from 1948 until 1970. In addition, he had made his name on the battlefield in World War I, where he was awarded the Military Cross, and he became a Knight of the British Empire in 1959. He married Dorothy, the sister of his one-time political rival, the Labour leader Hugh Gaitskell. His brother Claude captained England against Northern Ireland in 1925.

MONDAY 18TH JUNE 2001

Alvin Bubb, a striker who was born in Paddington in October 1980, joined Rovers from Queens Park Rangers, where he had enjoyed just nine minutes of league action. He played for Rovers in three (plus ten as substitute) league matches before moving to Billericay Town in August 2002. Though five feet four inches in height, it was with a header that he had his best chance of scoring for Rovers; his point-blank effort being spectacularly saved by Darlington's former Rovers goalkeeper Andy Collett. He and his brother Byron later joined Slough Town together, and he subsequently moved on to Aylesbury United and Wealdstone. Byron was to win one full international cap for Grenada against Guyana in February 2004, whilst a third brother, Bradley, was with Hendon in the 2004-05 season.

THURSDAY 19TH JUNE 1863

John Goodall was born in Westminster and helped Preston North End to the Football League and FA Cup double in 1888-89, also and also won 14 full caps for England. His many years in the game included spells in the Football League with Derby County, New Brighton Tower and Glossop as well as playing in France, Scotland and Wales. In March 1905, at the age of 41 years 283 days, he scored for Watford against Rovers in the Southern League to become the oldest goalscorer in any competitive match featuring Rovers. Despite his goal, Watford lost this game 3-1 in front of an Eastville crowd of 6,000, with Andy Smith scoring twice for Rovers and Billy Clark once.

WEDNESDAY 20TH JUNE 1866

As the holder of four full England caps, George Kinsey, who was born in June 1866 in Burton-upon-Trent, was well known to Victorian football supporters. The fact that he signed for Rovers, at the end of a long career with Burton Swifts, Wolves, Aston Villa, Derby County and Notts County, was a real feather in the club's cap. The eldest child to Jabez and Elizabeth Kinsey, his father being a brewer's assistant from Leicestershire, George Kinsey married Rosa Butler and had a daughter Elizabeth. He had won an FA Cup winner's medal in 1893, with Wolves, and played in 92 games for Rovers between 1897 and 1900, scoring ten goals.

TUESDAY 21st JUNE 1966

Bob Bloomer, who played as a full-back for Rovers in eleven (plus eleven more as substitute) league matches between 1990 and 1992, was born in Sheffield. In five years at Chesterfield, Bloomer had accumulated 120 (plus 21 as substitute) league appearances and had scored 15 times prior to his arrival at Twerton Park in March 1990 in a £20,000 deal. After Rovers' promotion to Division Two he was used in the side, even playing in goal when Brian Parkin was injured in an FA Cup tie against Crewe Alexandra in January 1991. Bloomer moved to Cheltenham Town in August 1992, thus beginning a long association until March 2009 with the Whaddon Road side.

SUNDAY 22nd JUNE 1947

Geoff Fox, a full-back who was to give Rovers excellent service over eight seasons, signed from Ipswich Town on a free transfer. Though born in Bristol in January 1925, Fox had made his league bow at Portman Road and returned to his home town to play in 274 league matches for Rovers. He was credited with an own goal when Rovers lost to Newcastle United in 1951 in the club's first-ever FA Cup quarter-final, but he recovered to play in 110 consecutive league games as Rovers were crowned Division Three (South) champions in 1952-53. One of Fox's two goals for Rovers came in the first game in Division Two. He also played for Swindon Town, enjoyed Minor Counties cricket with Suffolk, and died on a Worcestershire golf course on New Year's Day 1994.

SUNDAY 23rd JUNE 1918

Ray Warren, the only player whose first and last league appearances for Rovers were more than 20 years apart, was born in Bristol. The epitome of the one-club footballer, Warren was an amateur with Rovers from 1934, signed professional forms when making his debut in March 1936 and played exactly 450 times for the club in the league, scoring 28 times from centre-half, before retiring in 1956. Had war not intervened, this impressively long career might have included even more appearances. As it was, Warren was an ever-present in five seasons and captained his side to the Third Division (South) championship in 1952-53. He died in Bristol in March 1988, aged 69.

SATURDAY 24TH JUNE 1899

George Pither, who played twice for Rovers in the 1924-25 season at outside-left, was born in Kew. Although he had previously played at Eastville with both Brentford and Millwall, he never turned out there in a Rovers shirt, as his two games were both away fixtures. Later with Torquay United, Merthyr Town, Liverpool, Crewe Alexandra and New Brighton – representing all these sides in the Football League – Pither moved to non-league football in Kent and died in Tunbridge Wells in January 1966.

SATURDAY 25TH JUNE 1960

Graham Muxworthy, who had earlier played twice in the league for Crystal Palace, joined Rovers in a £1,000 deal from Chippenham Town. A Bristol-born 21-year-old outside-left, he was to play for Rovers in eight consecutive league matches, all of them in April 1963, before playing for Bridgwater Town, Glastonbury, Bath City, Salisbury City, Weston-super-Mare and Minehead. He was a youth team coach at Rovers in the early 1990s and Academy coach at Bristol City thereafter.

SATURDAY 26TH JUNE 1909

Amid great celebrations, Innox Park, later renamed Twerton Park, was opened in Bath on land donated by Thomas Carr of Poolemeade, West Twerton. The ceremony began at 3pm and featured a procession of scholars, the singing of hymns and a speech given by Robert Hope, a pattern maker of Maybrick Road, South Twerton, who was chairman of the parish council. There were festivities all day, much enjoyed by young and old in the local community. Rovers were to play home games at Twerton Park, Bath between 1986 and 1996.

THURSDAY 27TH JUNE 1929

John Cook, who played twice for Rovers in the first post-war league season, was born in Iron Acton, near Bristol. A brother-in-law of his Rovers team-mate Cliff Baker, Cook signed for Rovers from Coalpit Heath in September 1946 and played twice in the league as well as in the shock FA Cup defeat away to non-league Merthyr Town. He remained on Rovers' books until 1952 before joining Bridgwater Town as a professional where his career was ended by a broken leg sustained against Dorchester Town in February 1953.

FRIDAY 28TH JUNE 1929

Wally Gillespie, a sturdy 25-year-old full-back from Fife, joined Bristol Rovers in a £300 deal from Newcastle United. Gillespie had previously played for East Fife, for whom he played in the Scottish Cup Final of 1927, before appearing in nine league games for the mighty Newcastle United side. He played just twice for Rovers before joining St. Mirren and later rejoining East Fife, for whom he played in an impressive tally of 356 Scottish League fixtures. He was a member of the Belfast Distillery side that reached the Irish Cup Final of 1933.

FRIDAY 29TH JUNE 1956

Jim Shervey, who was born in Merthyr Tydfil in the summer of 1882, died in Weston-super-Mare, at the age of 73. He had lived for many years in Parry's Lane in Westbury-on-Trym, Bristol and played Southern League football with Rovers between 1910 and 1914, running up a total of 50 appearances and 16 goals. In many respects, his greatest moments came in the FA Cup. He scored Rovers' opening goal in the shock victory over Notts County in 1913 and added both Rovers' goals in the 5-2 defeat twelve months later against the mighty Preston North End at Deepdale.

WEDNESDAY 30TH JUNE 1954

Peter Aitken, a key figure in the successful Rovers line-up of the 1970s and the only man to captain both Bristol sides in league action, was born in Penarth. A schoolboy on Rovers' books, he played in the league side from August 1972 until the summer of 1980, accumulating 230 (plus four as substitute) league games as a full-back or defensive midfielder. He scored three times. The winner of three Welsh under-23 caps, he helped Rovers to promotion to Division Two in 1973-74 and played in the first six years back in the second tier of English football. At Bristol City, he was one of the 'Ashton Gate Eight', whose contracts were torn up in 1982 to save the club. Later with York City, he also played in Hong Kong and has since held down several coaching posts in and around the Bristol area, becoming Rovers' Community Officer in 2000.

BRISTOL ROVERS
On This Day

JULY

MONDAY 1st JULY 2002

Adam Barrett, a central defender, joined Rovers on a free transfer from Mansfield Town. Born in Dagenham in November 1979, Barrett had been on Orient's books before playing regularly at both Plymouth Argyle and Mansfield. He was appointed Rovers' captain and scored five goals in 90 league appearances. Barrett joined Southend United in June 2004 and has since enjoyed many successful seasons with his new club.

FRIDAY 2nd JULY 1965

Wally Hammond, who had scored two goals in 19 league matches for Rovers between 1921 and 1924, died in Durban, South Africa at the age of 62. In April 1933 he had set a new world record in scoring 336 not out, whilst playing cricket for England against New Zealand; an innings of just 318 minutes that included ten sixes, three off successive balls at one point, and 34 fours. Hammond scored 7,249 runs in 85 Test matches for England at an average of 58.45 runs and represented Gloucestershire between 1920 and 1951.

FRIDAY 3rd JULY 1908

Alf Robertson, a six-feet-tall goalkeeper who played in eight league matches for Rovers in the 1935-36 season, was born in Sunderland. A former worker in the shipbuilding industry, Robertson had represented Bradford Park Avenue and Orient in the league prior to his arrival at Eastville and he was to concede four goals at Crystal Palace and four more at home to Reading whilst with Rovers. Joining Accrington Stanley in June 1936, he was a regular up to the outbreak of war. He died in Clayton-le-Moors in September 1984, at the age of 76.

FRIDAY 3rd JULY 1970

Signing from Sheffield Wednesday, winger Gordon Fearnley was born in Bradford in January 1950 but made his name as part of Rovers' 1973-74 promotion side. In seven years with Rovers, he scored 21 goals in 95 (plus 26 as substitute) league appearances, leaving in 1977 to play in North America with Miami Toros, Toronto Blizzard and Fort Lauderdale Strikers. Fearnley, whose brother and father played in rugby league finals at Wembley, is now a lawyer in America.

MONDAY 4TH JULY 1966

John Scales, a future England international who played for Rovers between 1985 and 1987, was born in Harrogate. A central defender or full-back with Rovers, he arrived from Leeds United and scored twice in 68 (plus four as substitute) league matches. A July 1987 move to Wimbledon enabled him to play in the 1988 FA Cup final, in which the Dons shocked the footballing world by defeating Liverpool 1-0. A £3,000,000 move to Liverpool preceded a League Cup winner's medal, three England caps and a short spell at both Spurs and Ipswich Town.

SATURDAY 5TH JULY 1980

Archie Young, who played as a wing-half for the Pirates in 24 league matches during the season the club conceded 95 league goals, died in Exmouth, aged 73. Born in Twechar, near Dumbarton in December 1906, Young played for Dunfermline Athletic, before making his Leicester City debut in an 8-2 defeat against Arsenal. Joining Rovers in July 1935, he was in the side defeated 12-0 at Luton Town on Easter Monday 1936 and later played for Exeter City, Gillingham and Rochdale.

FRIDAY 6TH JULY 1990

Peter Cawley, a tall central defender, left Rovers to sign for Southend United. Born in Walton-on-Thames in September 1965, Cawley had played for Wimbledon and Fulham before joining Rovers, initially on loan. He played in ten (plus three as substitute) league matches in two seasons at Twerton Park. He was to play in six (plus one as substitute) league games for Southend United, scoring once, before representing Exeter City, Barnet and Colchester United.

FRIDAY 7TH JULY 1972

The death in Bristol of Bert Tann marked the end of an era in Rovers' history. Born in Plaistow in 1914, one of eleven children to a ship's painter, Tann had played as a wing-half at Charlton Athletic before managing Rovers from January 1950 to April 1968. During those years, Rovers gained promotion for the first time to Division Two and reached two FA Cup quarter-finals. He was awarded a medal by the Football Association in 1971 to mark 21 years' service for one club.

WEDNESDAY 8TH JULY 1942

Bernard Hall, who played in 163 league games in goal for Rovers, was born in Bath. Formerly with Twerton Youth Club, Hall joined Rovers at the age of 16 and signed professional forms a year later. Short for a goalkeeper, he was fearless, brave and strong. From April 1963, with Rovers having been relegated to Division Three, to November 1965, he appeared in 115 consecutive league matches for the Eastville club. However, a head injury suffered against Middlesbrough on New Year's Eve 1966 left him in a coma for several days and forced his early retirement.

SATURDAY 9TH JULY 1927

Peter Sampson, who played for Rovers in 339 league matches through the club's halcyon days of the 1950s, was born in Great Watering in Essex. Once with Devizes Town, Sampson was a committed wing-half, who defended in depth and scored just three goals in his long career. A debut in August 1948 was followed by three years as an ever-present, his run of 143 consecutive league matches encompassed the 1952-53 Third Division (South) championship season. Leaving Rovers in July 1961, Sampson later captained Trowbridge Town for two seasons and worked as a milkman in Soundwell, Bristol. He died in May 2009.

WEDNESDAY 10TH JULY 1968

In 24 hours, five inches of rain fell in Eastville and the stadium was flooded. The fire brigade was called and they pumped out five million gallons of water. Across the Bristol area, the flooding caused chaos at the start of July 1968 and sadly there were eight fatalities, three of whom were washed away in a car in Keynsham.

FRIDAY 11TH JULY 1952

George Chance, an erstwhile professional athlete who played for Rovers in the early 1920s, died in Quarry Bank, Staffordshire, aged 55. Stourbridge-born, he joined Rovers in May 1920 and scored eleven times in 80 league appearances as an outside-right before moving to rivals Gillingham in a £100 move in June 1924. He later won a Third Division (South) championship medal at Millwall, before retiring in 1930 to run a public house in the Midlands.

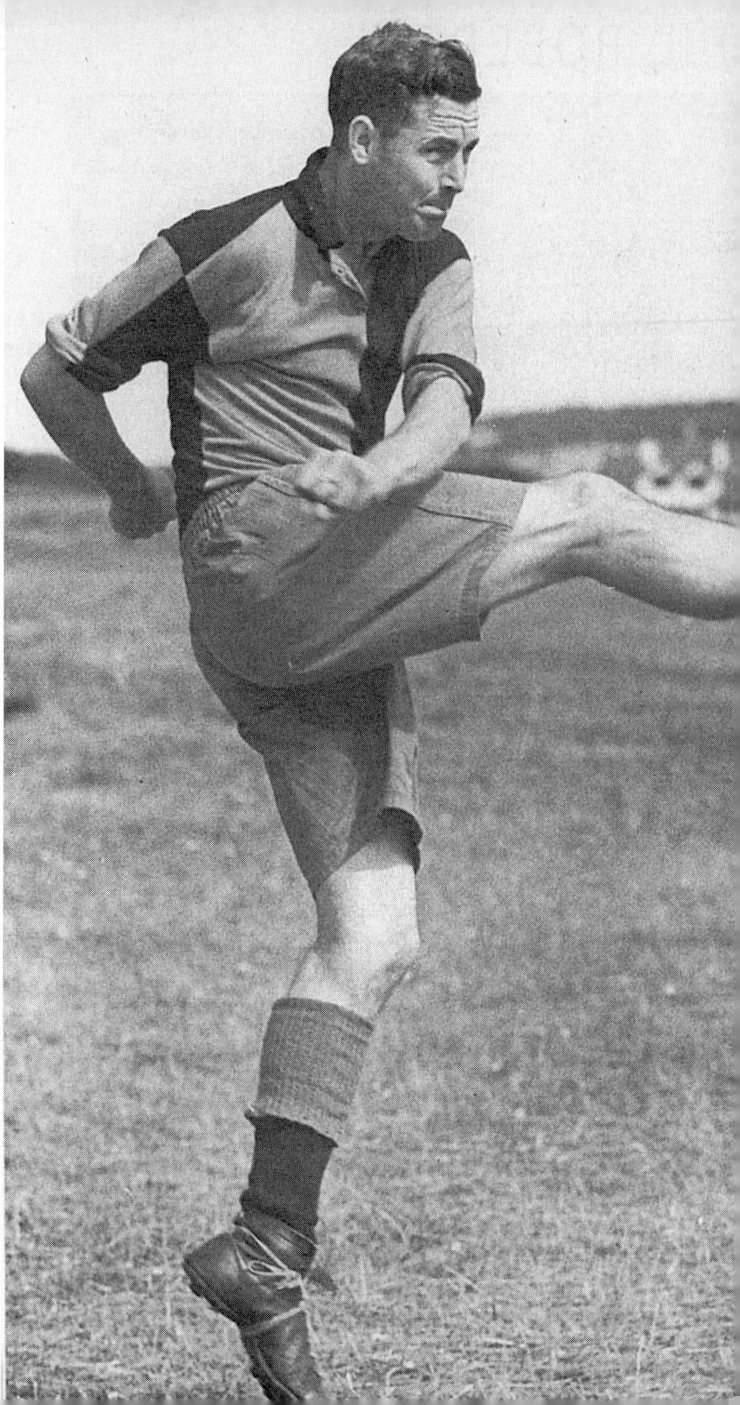

PETER SAMPSON WAS BORN IN JULY 1927

WEDNESDAY 12TH JULY 1944

Terry Cooper was born at Brotherton, near Castleford. A fast, raiding full-back who won 20 England caps and starred in Leeds United's golden era through the 1970s, Cooper played for Middlesbrough and Bristol City before joining Rovers in August 1979. He started 53 league matches for the club and appeared as substitute in five more. Appointed player-manager in April 1980, he was in charge when Rovers suffered relegation to Division Three in 1980-81 and was dismissed in October 1981. Thereafter, he played for Doncaster Rovers and was manager at Bristol City, Exeter City and Birmingham City.

WEDNESDAY 12TH JULY 1978

Few players have enjoyed as brief a career at Rovers as Ryan Morgan, who was born in Bristol. Tall and strong in the tackle, Morgan was a left-footed midfielder who captained the youth side, but played just one league game, against Watford in March 1997. He later played for Lebeq Tavern and Bishop Sutton.

THURSDAY 13TH JULY 1978

Marcus Andreasson, who scored one of Rovers' three first-half goals at Swindon Town in October 2000, was born in Buchanan, Liberia. His Swedish father moved the family to his native country in 1981 and they settled in Vaxjo. A very tall central defender, Andreasson played for Kosta and Östers before signing for Rovers in July 1998. He scored just the one goal in 14 (plus one as substitute) league matches in two spells with Rovers, later playing for Kalmar FF and Bryne FK. He was in the Molde FK side that defeated Lillestrom 4-2 in the Norwegian Cup final of 2005.

MONDAY 14TH JULY 1915

Sites of massacres are not generally places of birth of footballers, but James Durkan, born at Bannockburn, where Edward II had been defeated and repelled by Robert the Bruce in 1314, played for Rovers in two league matches in 1935. In a similar vein, Donnie Gillies, a Bristol City stalwart who gave Rovers two seasons' service at the end of his career in the 1980s, was born in June 1951 at Glencoe, where the Campbells had instigated a celebrated massacre in February 1692.

TUESDAY 14TH JULY 1915

A clever winger with a fine goalscoring record, Charlie Wipfler was born in Trowbridge. He contributed five goals in 18 league fixtures in the 1934-35 season, before two years with Heart of Midlothian that included a goal on his debut against Partick Thistle and two more in their 8-3 local derby victory over Hibernian. Later with Watford both sides of World War II, Wipfler died in Petts Wood, Kent in June 1983 at the age of 68.

MONDAY 15TH JULY 1930

Brian Doyle, a full-back who played in 43 league games for Rovers between January 1958 and the summer of 1960, scoring once, was born in Manchester. A Cheshire County defender, Doyle played for Stoke City and Exeter City prior to his time at Eastville. Signing for Rovers in June 1957, he retired in 1960 to train Rovers' colts. Later a fully-qualified Football Association coach, he was manager at Workington and Stockport County, assistant at Blackpool and coached in Kuwait and Finland. He died in Blackpool in December 1992, aged 62.

SATURDAY 16TH JULY 1932

No one could have foreseen the importance of the first greyhound racing at Eastville Stadium. At first, this was a shrewd way of making money but, in March 1940, with Rovers in severe financial straits, the Eastville ground was sold to the racing company for £12,000. Following the South Stand fire of 1980, Rovers' future at the ground looked bleaker still and the club's final game at their spiritual home came against Chesterfield in April 1986.

SUNDAY 17TH JULY 1960

Tom Boucher, a forward who scored ten goals in 27 Southern League matches for Rovers in the 1900-01 season, died in Sodbury. Born in Worcestershire in 1879, the second of six children to a wheelwright, Boucher was with Notts County before joining Bedminster, one of the clubs that made up Bristol City, in 1899. He scored against Rovers in the Southern League in the 1899-1900 season and signed for the club in May 1900. After leaving Rovers, he played for what is now Bristol City, before joining New Brompton, the modern-day Gillingham, in 1903.

MONDAY 18TH JULY 1927

Geoff Bradford, the only Rovers player to play for England, was born in Clifton, Bristol. Bradford's tally of 242 goals in 461 league matches between 1949 and 1964 remains an all-time club record, one that is unlikely to be surpassed. Such form helped his club to an unprecedented promotion to the second tier of English football and two FA Cup quarter-finals; it also earned him a call-up to play for England in Denmark in October 1955, where he scored in a 5-1 victory. His ratio of a goal every two games over 15 seasons was achieved through his excellent technique and his gift of a very powerful shot with either foot, as well as his reluctance to give in. Bradford later worked locally for an oil company and died in Bristol in December 1994, aged 67.

WEDNESDAY 19TH JULY 1989

Les Golledge, who scored the thousandth goal Rovers scored in the Football League, died in Fishponds, Bristol, at the age of 77. Born in Chipping Sodbury in August 1911, Golledge was to score just the one goal, in a 6-1 win at home to Exeter City in April 1936, in his nine league appearances for Rovers. Having played in Division Two with Bristol City, he signed for Rovers in June 1935 and left for a fruitless spell at Lincoln City from the summer of 1937. He was with Bristol St. George for many years, including twelve as trainer and eight as chairman.

THURSDAY 20TH JULY 1939

Albert Turner – who had scored four times in 21 league games for Rovers in the final season prior to World War II – joined Bath City, bringing to an end his seven-month spell on Rovers' books. Born in Sheffield in September 1907, Turner had played for Hull City, Doncaster Rovers and Walsall before joining Rovers on a free transfer from Cardiff City in December 1938. An outside-left, he contributed greatly to the struggle to retain league status as war clouds hovered over Europe. He scored his 99th and final league goal in the 1-1 draw with Bristol City in February 1939. His son Gordon Turner was a well-known player in league circles during the 1950s, representing Luton Town in over 400 matches.

MONDAY 21st JULY 1947

Ray Graydon – who scored 33 league goals in 129 (plus two as substitute) appearances as a flying winger between 1965 and 1971 – was born in Bristol. Fair-haired, fast and popular with fans, he furthered his football career at Aston Villa, Coventry City and Oxford United. In April 2002, having managed Walsall, he returned to Rovers, but his spell as manager coincided with the club being marooned in the basement division and he left in January 2004 to take up coaching posts, first in China and later with Leicester City.

TUESDAY 22nd JULY 1947

A veteran of pre-war league football with both Newport County and Ipswich Town, Fred Chadwick was 33 years old when he signed for Rovers. Born in Manchester in November 1913, he had scored six times in one wartime game for Norwich City, but managed just one goal in six league appearances at Eastville. That sole strike came against Brighton & Hove Albion on his club debut. He joined Street in August 1948 and continued to live in Bristol, where he died in September 1987, aged 73.

MONDAY 22nd JULY 1968

Bert Bennett, who totalled 101 Southern League games for Rovers between 1912 and 1915, died in Bristol at the age of 78. Though born in Oldbury-upon-Severn, he was a student at Thornbury Grammar School who was signed up by Rovers in January 1911 as a left-back. His greatest moment in a Rovers shirt was as part of the defence in January 1913 that held out for a clean sheet in the famous FA Cup win over First Division Notts County. When the Southern League was suspended in the midst of war in 1915, Bennett retired from football.

WEDNESDAY 23rd JULY 1986

Rovers' departure from Eastville caused many ructions and an emergency meeting was called of the Western League committee. This meeting resulted in Bath City reserves agreeing to play at Hambrook, Rovers' training ground, before joining Radstock Town in a ground-sharing scheme. Rovers' move to Twerton Park may have been inconvenient for the club and its fans, but it caused further changes down the ladder too.

MONDAY 24TH JULY 1972

Bobby Brown, who had scored four goals in 28 (plus seven as substitute) league matches for Rovers, joined Weymouth on a free transfer. An inside-forward who had been in and out of Rovers' side since scoring on his debut against Gillingham in December 1968, Bristol-born Brown had also spent time on loan with Newport County. Brown married a niece of Barry Watkins, once a Rovers full-back, and his cousin Judith married the former Rovers goalkeeper Richard Crabtree. He subsequently spent many seasons with Bath City, Gloucester City and Southern League Minehead, before coaching at Yate Town and Winterbourne.

THURSDAY 24TH JULY 2008

The second of three games on Rovers' pre-season tour to Sweden ended in a resounding 4-0 victory over Malmö Anadolu and a personal success for Joshua Klein-Davies, who scored all the tourists' goals. Rovers introduced Mike Green in goal and untried youngsters Tom Parrinello and James Fraser outfield and dominated from the start, with Klein-Davies giving Rovers a 19th-minute lead, and scoring three times after half-time, on 59, 80 and 83 minutes. Klein-Davies left Rovers in 2009 with two (plus eight as substitute) league games and one goal to his name.

THURSDAY 25TH JULY 1929

Paddy Leonard, who scored for Rovers in both Division Three (South) and Division Two, was born in Dublin. An inside-forward who joined Rovers from Bath City in July 1952, he scored twice in 14 league appearances, which encompassed promotion as champions, before joining Colchester United in June 1954. After one season at Layer Road and a further year with Tonbridge, Leonard moved back to Dublin, where he worked as a car salesman.

WEDNESDAY 26TH JULY 2000

Rovers equalled their record transfer fee received when Jason Roberts moved to West Bromwich Albion. The fee of £2,000,000 was the same as that received almost two years earlier when Fulham had signed another Rovers striker, Barry Hayles. Roberts had played in 73 (plus five as substitute) league games for Rovers, scoring 38 goals, between 1998 and 2000 and he went on to further his career in the top tier of English football.

TUESDAY 27th JULY 1896

Jack Thomson, an enthusiastic and brave goalkeeper, was born in Greenock. Six league outings with Rovers in the spring of 1922 preceded a career in England, Wales, Scotland and the United States of America. He "showed himself to be a custodian of considerable merit", purred the *Alloa Journal* in August 1922. Thomson died in Westchester in New York State in May 1980.

THURSDAY 27th JULY 1905

The first South American-born player to play and score against Rovers was Francisco Enrique Gonsalez, who was born in Vernado Tuerto, Argentina in July 1905. Upon emigrating to Britain, he took on the name Frank Peed and played for both Norwich City, in December 1930, and Newport County, scoring in November 1932, in league matches against Rovers. He died in 1967.

MONDAY 28th JULY 1997

Lee Zabek, born in Bristol in October 1978, signed for Rovers as a professional. A six-foot-tall midfielder, Zabek had represented Northavon Schools and his aerial strength and tough tackling earned him a place in the Rovers side. He headed home Barry Hayles' cross a minute from the end of the 1-1 draw with Millwall in April 1998 – his only goal in 21 (plus eight as substitute) league appearances for Rovers. Joining Exeter City in August 2000 on a free transfer, he later played for Clevedon Town, Keynsham Town and Wotton Rovers.

SUNDAY 29th JULY 1894

David Steele, who won league championship medals and Scottish caps after leaving Rovers, was born in Carluke, Lanarkshire. Formerly at St. Mirren, he joined Rovers in November 1919, helped the club into the Football League and played in Rovers' first ever league fixture, a 2-0 defeat at Millwall in August 1920. After 67 league matches and two goals, this former miner and powerful centre-half spent seven seasons at Huddersfield Town, who won three consecutive league titles in his years at Leeds Road. Winning three full caps for Scotland, Steele also played for Preston and Bury, coached in Denmark and was later manager at Huddersfield Town and both Bradford clubs. He died in Stanningley in May 1964.

SUNDAY 30TH JULY 1939

Graham Ricketts, who played for Rovers in 32 league games – without scoring – between February 1957 and the summer of 1961, was born in Oxford. A wing-half, Ricketts had made his debut at the age of 17 and went on to play league football for Stockport County, Doncaster Rovers and Peterborough United, before joining King's Lynn in 1970. Now retired, he lives in the Northampton area.

WEDNESDAY 31st JULY 1935

Having won a Welsh League championship with Llanelli, George Crisp signed for Rovers on the back of eight league games with Coventry City. He was to play in 22 league games with Rovers, scoring four goals from outside-left. Short and fast, he contributed one of the goals on his debut as Bristol City were defeated 2-0 at Ashton Gate in September 1935, but was also in the side that lost 12-0 at Luton Town later that campaign. Crisp joined Newport County in the summer of 1936. Later with Colchester United and Nottingham Forest, he scored one of Merthyr's three goals as they knocked Rovers out of the FA Cup in November 1946. Born in Pontypool in June 1911, George Crisp died in Penrhiwceiber in March 1982, aged 70.

WEDNESDAY 31st JULY 1991

Ernie Whatmore, a tough, balding centre-forward who scored hat-tricks for Rovers against Crystal Palace and Charlton Athletic, died in a Kidderminster nursing home at the age of 91. Born in Kidderminster in April 1900, Whatmore had won a Shropshire Senior Cup winner's medal with Shrewsbury Town before joining Rovers in July 1923. He scored 40 league goals in his 134 matches with Rovers and proved himself to be a popular leader of the attack. He moved to Queens Park Rangers in June 1928, scoring against Rovers before dropping into non-league football in 1933.

BRISTOL ROVERS
On This Day

AUGUST

TUESDAY 1st AUGUST 1972

In a 3-2 win at Trowbridge Town in a pre-season friendly, Rovers gave a game to 15-year-old Wayne Powell and the young striker responded with a goal. Born in October 1956, Powell made his league bow at the age of 18 and his ten league goals in 25 (plus seven as substitute) league matches included a Second Division hat-trick against Sheffield United. He later worked as a youth coach at Swansea City and Rovers, whilst his son Lewis was later also on Rovers' books.

WEDNESDAY 2nd AUGUST 1972

Having qualified for the Watney Cup, a tournament that rewarded the league's highest scoring clubs, Rovers reached the final by defeating First Division Burnley 2-0 at Turf Moor. This result was arguably more startling than the 2-0 victory at home to Wolves in the previous round. Frankie Prince and Bruce Bannister scored in front of a crowd of 10,589 to set up an ultimately successful final against Sheffield United to be held three days later at Eastville.

SATURDAY 3rd AUGUST 2002

Ronnie Maugé, a midfielder who was born in Islington in September 1970 and played in 50 (plus three as substitute) league matches without scoring for Rovers, was sold to St. Albans City. Previously with Fulham, Bury, Manchester City and Plymouth Argyle, for whom he scored at Wembley, Maugé was instrumental in Rovers' ultimately unsuccessful promotion push in 1999-2000 and an injury sustained in international football for Trinidad and Tobago ruled the central midfielder out of the end of that season. He later played for Aldershot Town and Whitton United.

WEDNESDAY 4th AUGUST 1971

The broadcaster David Icke, who famously declared himself to be the 'Son of God', played in goal for Hereford United reserves in their 1-1 draw with their Rovers counterparts at Edgar Street. Having spent two years with Coventry City, Icke had joined Hereford United that week and was beaten by Mike Green's shot after 40 minutes. After Wayne Jones hit a post, both he and Sandy Allan saw their shots saved by Icke, before the home side equalised through Billy Meadows nine minutes from time.

SATURDAY 5TH AUGUST 1972

A crowd of 19,380 gathered at Eastville in sweltering heat for the Watney Cup Final between Rovers and First Division Sheffield United. The visitors fielded teenage goalkeeper Tom McAlister, later a Rovers player himself, and his fine display kept the final scoreless though many felt Rovers had deserved to win. The match went to a penalty shoot-out. The first 13 penalties were scored and, with Dick Sheppard saving a crucial spot kick from the veteran Ted Hemsley, a survivor of Shrewsbury Town's 7-2 win over Rovers a decade earlier, Rovers recorded a 7-6 win. In only his third game in charge, manager Don Megson had led the club to its first major cup tournament win since 1935.

SATURDAY 5TH AUGUST 1978

Rovers only won once in six games in the Anglo-Scottish Cup and the darkest day for the club was the 6-1 defeat at the hands of their old rivals at Ashton Gate. Rovers' goal, in front of a crowd of 9,874, came from Gary Clarke who appeared in three games in this tournament prior to making his Football League debut. Tom Ritchie scored twice for Bristol City, whose other goals came from a Peter Cormack penalty, Chris Garland, Trevor Tainton and Clive Whitehead.

THURSDAY 6TH AUGUST 1942

Jimmy Humes, a winger who played in two league games for Rovers in the 1962-63 season, was born in Carlisle. As a 19-year-old, he had been in the Preston side that defeated Rovers 1-0 at Deepdale in October 1961. He joined the club on a free transfer in June the following year on the recommendation of his former colleague, Eastville favourite Alfie Biggs. Humes later played league football for both Chester and Barnsley before retiring in 1968.

WEDNESDAY 7TH AUGUST 1900

Ernie Sambidge, a full-back with Rovers in the early 1920s, was born in Newcastle-upon-Tyne. Tall and strong in the tackle, he joined the Eastville side from Walker Celtic in May 1922 and appeared 23 times in the league before playing for Bath City, Street and Trowbridge Town. Settling locally, Sambidge died in Bristol in November 1979, aged 79.

SATURDAY 7TH AUGUST 1948

A single-goal defeat in Nijmegen heralded the start of Rovers' tour of the Netherlands, the goal coming in the second half. Twenty-four hours later, Rovers played Racing Club Haarlem, who were coached by Les Talbot, a former Rovers' reserves player. Three goals ahead by half-time, Rovers won 4-2, thanks to two goals from forward Vic Lambden and one apiece from Barry Watkins and Maurice Lockier.

WEDNESDAY 7TH AUGUST 1991

Both Rovers' full-backs were sent off in a Gloucestershire Cup tie before a crowd of 6,796 at Ashton Gate in which Bristol City defeated Rovers 3-2. Ian Alexander and Geoff Twentyman both received their marching orders as Rovers stumbled to defeat. Bob Taylor scored twice, and Rob Edwards once, for City, with Phil Purnell and David Mehew scoring for Rovers; all five goals in the 3-2 defeat were scored before half-time. The Gloucestershire Cup took place for 99 seasons before being axed later in the 1990s.

FRIDAY 8TH AUGUST 1890

Captain Albert Prince-Cox, who spent six years until October 1936 as Rovers' manager, was born in Southsea. A former footballer and boxer, who had refereed several Rovers games, Prince-Cox had refereed 32 internationals in 15 countries and once presented the king with his daily weather forecast. He arrived at Eastville in October 1930 in a red open-topped sports car, arranged overseas tours for the club, introduced the now-familiar quartered shirt and led Rovers to the Third Division (South) Cup final victory in 1935.

TUESDAY 8TH AUGUST 1916

The former Rovers player Walter Gerrish was killed in battle in Flanders, one of many professional sportsmen from many countries to perish in the Great War. Born in Bristol in December 1884, he had enjoyed local football before signing for Rovers in 1904. After 49 Southern League matches and eleven goals, he was transferred to Aston Villa in April 1909, where he won a league championship medal in 1910 before joining Preston North End and later Chesterfield. John Hardman and Joe Hulme were the other two former Rovers players who lost their lives on the battlefield in World War I.

SUNDAY 9TH AUGUST 1970

Lee Jones, who played in 76 league matches in goal for Rovers between March 1998 and the summer of 2000, was born in Pontypridd. Previously with Swansea City and briefly on loan at Crewe Alexandra, Jones joined Rovers in an exchange deal involving Julian Alsop and his form at Rovers earned a call-up to the Wales B squad. He was also one of four players, two from each side, sent off in the last minute of the draw at Gillingham in August 1998. Joining Stockport County in July 2000, he later played for Blackpool, Bury and Darlington before joining Nantwich Town in November 2007.

SATURDAY 10TH AUGUST 1901

Viv Gibbins, an amateur centre-forward who was Rovers' top scorer in the 1932-33 season was born in Forest Gate, London. The holder of two full caps as well as eight England amateur caps, Gibbins also played league football with West Ham United, Brentford and Southampton and joined Rovers in June 1932. He scored 14 goals in 37 league matches for Rovers, a tally that included two hat-tricks. Headmaster of a London school, he died in Herne Bay in November 1979, aged 78.

THURSDAY 11TH AUGUST 1966

Nigel Martyn, a tall Cornishman who played in goal in 101 league games for Rovers before winning 23 full England caps, was born in Bethel, near St. Austell. He joined Rovers from St. Blazey in August 1987 and left in November 1989 for Crystal Palace as Britain's first one-million-pound goalkeeper. Martyn played for Palace in the 1990 FA Cup final and represented Leeds United and Everton before retiring in 2006. He was an unused member of the England squad at two World Cup finals tournaments and one European championship.

TUESDAY 12TH AUGUST 1980

'Hartillery' attacks were the speciality of centre-forward Bill Hartill, who was born in Wolverhampton in July 1905 and died in Walsall at the age of 75. In 36 league games for Rovers, the robust forward scored 19 times. For many years Wolves' all-time top scorer, he also played for both Everton and Liverpool before running a pub in Wolverhampton.

SATURDAY 12TH AUGUST 1978

Rovers' season opened with a League Cup tie at home to Hereford United before a crowd of 5,001 at Eastville. The corner count of 17-0 in Rovers' favour illustrates clearly their superiority, yet only Peter Aitken's long-range drive after 25 minutes and David Staniforth's header ten minutes later served as tangible evidence. "We should have had six," Rovers' manager Bobby Gould stated afterwards. David Williams fired a late penalty over the bar, before David Jones' goal on 89 minutes from the visitors' best move of the game gave Hereford hope for the second leg, which they won 4-0 at Edgar Street.

TUESDAY 12TH AUGUST 1980

League Cup ties are often decided nowadays on penalty shoot-outs, but Rovers' first such experience in this competition came at Eastville when, after a 1-1 draw, Rovers defeated Exeter City 7-6 on penalties. Chic Bates had scored for Rovers, and Tony Kellow for the Grecians, when the initial game was drawn in Devon. The same two players scored again in the replay before Rovers were victorious.

SATURDAY 13TH AUGUST 1927

One early experiment with a white ball was Rovers' pre-season trial game in 1927. The annual fixture between the Whites and the Blues gave club and spectators the opportunity to view new signings and see what prospects the club would have for the forthcoming campaign. The experiment, though, was not a success as the paint soon peeled off the ball.

TUESDAY 14TH AUGUST 1984

Mickey Barrett's death of cancer at the age of only 24 stunned everyone connected with Rovers. Born in Bristol in September 1959, the popular and exciting winger had tormented defences for over four years and he was well respected in Division Three. He had played for Rovers in 119 (plus ten as substitute) league matches, scoring 18 goals. More than this, though, he had become a cult figure amongst an adoring home crowd at Eastville, a beacon of hope that Rovers could achieve great things in the years to come. Struggling in pre-season training, Barrett had gone to hospital for tests and his sudden death was an enormous shock.

TUESDAY 14TH AUGUST 2007

There are few players who have links with Serbia, Albania and Finland, but Shefki Kuqi is certainly one. Born in Serbia, he was in line to play international football for both Albania and Finland, opting for the latter. Rovers created a shock by defeating Championship side Crystal Palace in the Carling Cup at the Memorial Stadium. The game was drawn 1-1, after Craig Disley had equalised Palace's goal from Dougie Freedman, and Kuqi then hit the crossbar in the subsequent penalty shoot-out which Rovers won 4-1.

WEDNESDAY 15TH AUGUST 1962

George Reay, who scored nine goals in 67 league matches for Rovers in the late 1920s, died in York, aged 59. Born in East Howdon in 1903, Reay was an outside-right who had played league football with both South Shields and Reading before trying his luck north of the border with Raith Rovers. He joined Rovers in May 1928 and made the right-wing berth his own for two seasons, before joining Coventry City in July 1930.

SATURDAY 16TH AUGUST 1980

A few hours after Rovers had drawn 1-1 at home to Orient on the opening day of the new season, in which, before a crowd of 5,831, Rovers' David Williams and the visitors' John Chiedozie had traded goals in the opening 16 minutes, the South Stand at Eastville was destroyed by fire. The club's administrative offices and dressing rooms could not be saved and what was left of the South Stand, which had been designed as a 2,000-seater stand in 1924, had to be demolished. Rovers were to play their next three 'home' league games at Ashton Gate.

SATURDAY 17TH AUGUST 1991

Not once, but twice Rovers have recovered from a 3-0 deficit at home to Ipswich Town to draw 3-3. In February 1939, Rovers trailed by three goals after 65 minutes only to draw through two Frank Curran goals and one from Tommy Mills. Amazingly, in August 1991 history repeated itself, as Rovers, 3-0 down on the hour mark, earned an unlikely draw with two goals from Devon White and one from debutant Marcus Stewart.

FRIDAY 18TH AUGUST 1893

George Douglas, a short, skilful outside-right, who scored five goals in 45 league games for Rovers in the 1920s, was born in Stepney. Formerly the captain of the West Ham side that won the English Schools Shield in 1906-07, Douglas represented the England amateur side and played league football for Leicester City, Burnley and Oldham Athletic. Having scored Leicester's first ever goal in the Football League, he joined Rovers in August 1926 in a £100 deal and left in July 1928 to become player-manager at Tunbridge Wells Rangers. He died in Southborough, Kent in January 1979.

SATURDAY 19TH AUGUST 1961

An Anfield crowd of 19,438 witnessed Rovers' opening game of the new season and saw Rovers' debutant right-back John Hills score an own goal after 65 minutes. Kevin Lewis scored the other as Liverpool won 2-0. Hills' feat of conceding an own goal in his first game was equalled by Sonny Parker, when he scored an own goal just 17 minutes into his debut against Cambridge United in December 2002.

SATURDAY 19TH AUGUST 1995

Scott Heggs and Steve Torpey were both sent off as Swansea City ended up with nine men at Twerton Park, yet still escaped with a point from a 2-2 draw. The crowd of 6,689 saw Gareth Taylor score twice for Rovers; Steve Torpey and Mike Basham replied for the Swans. While Torpey went on to play for Bristol City, Heggs had been on loan at Rovers the previous season, scoring once in two starts and three substitute appearances.

THURSDAY 20TH AUGUST 1953

Having waited so many years, Rovers' first ever Second Division fixture finished in a 4-4 draw, the first of eight occasions that Rovers have featured in a league game that has finished with this score. In predictable fashion, it was the ubiquitous Geoff Bradford who opened the scoring after 13 minutes and marked the occasion with a hat-trick, while Geoff Fox scored the other goal four minutes after half-time. Bobby Robson scored the first two of Fulham's three equalisers, with Arthur Stevens and Johnny Haynes also scoring before a Craven Cottage crowd of 25,000.

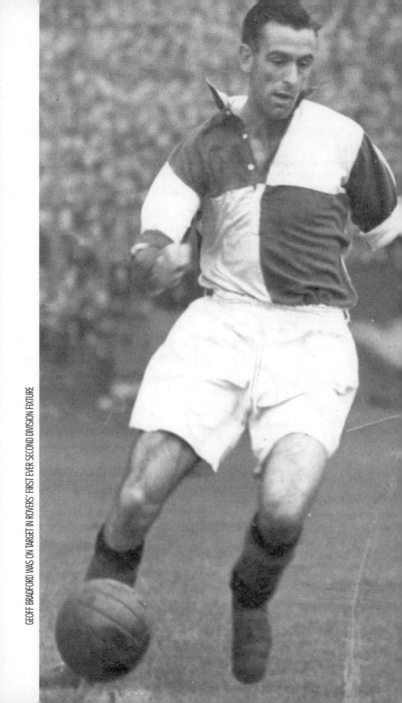

SATURDAY 21st AUGUST 1965

A change in league rules enabled teams to nominate a substitute from the start of the 1965-66 season and, for the opening game of the campaign, Rovers named the veteran wing-half Roy McCrohan as their spare man. He remained unused throughout the 1-1 draw at Grimsby, in which Bobby Jones scored for Rovers. Matt Tees added the goal for the Mariners, who also did not use their substitute. McCrohan was to appear ten times in Rovers' colours, adding one goal, before a summer 1966 move took him to Crawley Town.

SATURDAY 21st AUGUST 1971

Sandy Allan became only the third Rovers player to score two penalties in a league fixture, when his two spot kicks helped Rovers defeat Tranmere 2-1 at Eastville. Rovers were unchanged following a goalless draw at York City on the opening day of the season, though the visitors replaced the veteran Alan King with Paul Crossley and a crowd of 10,258 gathered at Eastville. Ray Mathias scored Tranmere's goal.

SATURDAY 22nd AUGUST 1998

Goalless draws can be exciting or drab, but one such game seemed to fill both criteria. Petering out into a scoreless draw of few chances, Rovers' game at Gillingham before 4,896 spectators exploded into life in the very last minute when a foul on Rovers' Stéphane Léoni sparked a mass brawl involving every player except the home side's goalkeeper Vince Bartram. Referee Matt Messias sent off two players from each side, Rovers' goalkeeper Lee Jones and full-back Trevor Challis as well as home defenders Barry Ashby and Adrian Pennock.

SATURDAY 23rd AUGUST 1997

When Gary Penrice scored Rovers' third goal against Carlisle United at the Memorial Stadium, he became the only player to have scored for the club on all four grounds on which Rovers have played 'home' fixtures. He scored for the first time at Eastville against York City in May 1985, fired home another against Swindon Town at Ashton Gate over Easter 1987 and added goals in four consecutive seasons at Twerton Park. Penrice became a firm favourite at Rovers, contributing 60 goals in almost 200 first-team games.

SATURDAY 23RD AUGUST 2008

The new season was kick-started into life as six well-taken goals signalled Rovers' intentions; Hereford United were defeated 6-1 before a crowd of 6,735 at the Memorial Stadium. Two goals up inside six minutes through new signing Darryl Duffy and Rickie Lambert, Rovers contributed three goals in each half, with the visitors responding through Steve Guinan in injury time. Duffy and Lambert scored two each, with Jeff Hughes – with an unstoppable shot – and Chris Lines, from a 30-yard free kick two minutes from time that went in off the bar, also scoring. Rovers' season was to prove the critics wrong, with Lambert contributing 29 of the side's 79 league strikes.

WEDNESDAY 24TH AUGUST 1938

Joe Davis, a central defender who played in 210 (plus one as substitute) league matches for Rovers and scored four goals, all of them penalties, was born in Bristol. Davis joined Rovers in March 1956 from local club Soundwell and was club captain as well as Player of the Year in 1964-65. A cousin of Bobby Jones, Davis was naturally right-footed but worked so hard on improving his left foot that it was with this so-called 'weaker' foot that he scored all his goals, all from the penalty spot. Later with Swansea Town, Davis coached for Rovers and worked for the *Bristol Evening Post* newspaper. Having not scored in his first 125 league matches for Rovers, Davis was entrusted with a penalty in the cauldron of a local derby at Ashton Gate, which he successfully converted.

SATURDAY 25TH AUGUST 1934

A founder member of the club, Richard Cater Conyers, who was born in Cirencester in 1864, died in Hayle, Cornwall. The fifth of eight children to Richard and Elizabeth Conyers, he was a printer by trade and, married to Edith Green, had a son and a daughter. Conyers was a centre-half who was a regular for the team in the first two years, from 1883 to 1885, when he was living in Frenchay Villas, St. George. It is known that he played in the first three Rovers games for which a line-up is traceable. Later chairman of the Southern League, he oversaw Rovers' admission to that league before moving to Cornwall later in life.

TUESDAY 25TH AUGUST 1936

Beating Bristol City always creates a warm feeling for any supporter of Bristol Rovers. In August 1936, Rovers defeated City at cricket, though it must be added that Rovers were fortunate at that time to boast an excellent pair of opening batsmen in Allan Murray and the Somerset cricketer Newman Bunce on their books. In September 1952 the former Rovers full-back Charles Littlewood organised a cricket match between Rovers and the Duke of Beaufort's XI. The Duke's side scored 164 all out, whilst Rovers scored 75-5, Ronnie Dix scoring 23.

SATURDAY 26TH AUGUST 1933

To any true supporter of Bristol Rovers, there can hardly be a better way to start a new season than to win 3-0 away to rivals Bristol City at Ashton Gate. Northern Irishman Jimmy McCambridge had joined the club from Ballymena United over the summer and he marked his debut with a hat-trick of headers, as Rovers got the campaign off to an excellent start. Only Joe Riley and Bobby Gould have also scored a hat-trick on their Rovers league debut.

WEDNESDAY 27TH AUGUST 1981

The death of Fred Leamon, Rovers' top scorer in the first post-war Football League season, cast a slight shadow over royal wedding celebrations. Jersey-born Leamon, who had served in the Marines during World War II, was working as a security man at the wedding of the Prince and Princess of Wales, Charles and Diana, when he suffered a heart attack at St Paul's Cathedral; he died a few weeks later.

SATURDAY 28TH AUGUST 1920

With the Southern League elected en masse to the Football League in 1920, Rovers lost 2-0 at Millwall in their inaugural match. A crowd of 25,000 at The Den saw Rovers lose to two second-half goals. First, 'Banger' Voisey scored from the edge of the area after 52 minutes, then goalkeeper Harry Stansfield lost the flight of the ball in the sun seven minutes later and Jimmy Broad headed home the second. Rovers also featured in the final league game ever played at The Den, winning 3-0 in May 1993.

THURSDAY 29TH AUGUST 1867

Harry Horsey served Rovers for 55 years, as a player, board member and chairman. Born in August 1867 in Eastville, he was a founder member of the club and is known to have played in at least 28 games, scoring twice, many of these alongside his younger brother, Bob, between 1883 and 1900. The oldest of eight children to Henry and Jane Horsey, he was sent to Colston's School before taking up work as a commercial clerk and director to a company making matches. He was married to Alice Mountain and they had a daughter, Ethel. Harry Horsey died in Bristol in July 1938.

MONDAY 29TH AUGUST 1960

In an astonishing game, Rovers recovered from four goals down to draw with Leeds United at Eastville. A crowd of 19,028 saw Leeds race to a 4-0 lead by half-time, through Colin Grainger, John Hawksby (2) and John McCole. Referee Jack Taylor, who later refereed the 1974 World Cup final, witnessed a Rovers revival with goals from George Petherbridge, Ian Hamilton and Peter Hooper (2) earning an unlikely point. As the game finished, it was Rovers pushing for what would have been an unlikely winning goal. Understandably, no other Rovers game has seen a side fail to win after running up a four-goal lead.

SATURDAY 30TH AUGUST 1924

Syd Holcroft's goal before an Eastville crowd of 8,000 was enough to defeat Merthyr Town in the first league game played in front of the newly-opened South Stand. This new structure ran the entire length of the touchline and seated 2,000 spectators. It had been built to replace an old 500-seater stand, complete with directors' box, which dated back to the days prior to Rovers' purchase of the Eastville Stadium in 1897.

WEDNESDAY 30TH AUGUST 1933

A home defeat at the hands of Crystal Palace lent a sense of reality to Rovers' ambitious pre-season hopes. A bumper crowd of 17,657 saw Rovers call up Jimmy Smith and George McNestry in place of Jack Eyres and Albert Taylor, but the side lost to a second-half goal from Palace's free-scoring centre-forward Peter Simpson.

MONDAY 30TH AUGUST 1948

A poor start to the season of three straight defeats was soon forgotten, as Rovers defeated Bournemouth 4-0 at Eastville to register the first points of the new campaign. In the absence of Fred Laing, Len Hodges returned to the side at inside-right and he added the fourth goal, after one from George Petherbridge and two from inside-left Jimmy Morgan had put Rovers in charge. There was a crowd of 14,121 at this Division Three (South) game.

SATURDAY 30TH AUGUST 1986

Following an enforced exiled from Bristol that was to last a decade, Rovers played their first league game at Twerton Park and defeated Bolton Wanderers 1-0. Rovers' goal came after 17 minutes, when a foul on Trevor Morgan by Mark Came resulted in a penalty that Morgan scored with some ease. Rovers held on to their lead, despite the sending-off of Nicky Tanner, to send the crowd of 4,092 home happy.

SATURDAY 31ST AUGUST 1996

After a decade away, Rovers played their first home game in Bristol when Stockport County were the first league side to visit the Memorial Ground. "It's the best thing since sliced bread," said Gordon Pearce. Lee Archer scored the first league goal on the ground after only twelve minutes, in front of a crowd of 6,380. The visitors, who had evidently not read the script, equalised 17 minutes from time through substitute John Jeffers to earn a 1-1 draw.

BRISTOL ROVERS
On This Day

SEPTEMBER

WEDNESDAY 1st SEPTEMBER 1920

Ellis Crompton scored Bristol Rovers' first ever Football League goal. Having lost 2-0 at Millwall in their opening league match, Rovers hosted Newport County at Eastville and recorded a 3-2 victory. The crowd was registered as 10,000. Crompton had the distinction of becoming the club's first goalscorer in league action, with Joe Norton and Steve Sims also finding their way onto the score-sheet. Newport, who trailed 2-0 at the interval, rallied with a strike from the veteran Arthur Wolstenholme and an Andy Walker penalty.

SATURDAY 2nd SEPTEMBER 1933

A carnival queen kicked off Rovers reserves' fixture at Taunton Town in the Western League. Madge Coles had been elected to the post of Taunton Carnival Queen and she started proceedings in a game that Rovers reserves led 4-2 at half-time, having been three goals up inside 15 minutes. The final score was 7-3, with George Berry, Phil Taylor (2), Jimmy Watson (2) and George Tadman (2) scoring for the reserves, Murley, Cookson and Curtis for Taunton Town.

WEDNESDAY 2nd SEPTEMBER 1992

Rovers' first game in the Anglo-Italian Cup was at Upton Park against a West Ham United side which led 1-0 at the break. With Julian Dicks scoring twice for the Hammers and Marcus Stewart twice for Rovers, before a crowd of 4,809, the sides drew 2-2. Rovers later also played Southend United in the competition, whilst the former Rovers striker Devon White scored the winning goal of the 1995 Anglo-Italian Cup Final at Wembley, when Notts County beat Ascoli 2-1.

SUNDAY 3rd SEPTEMBER 1978

Ted Hough, who had been transferred to Southampton in October 1921 for a fee of 52 pints of beer, died in Birmingham at the age of 78. A full-back who was born in Walsall in December 1899, Hough played in 175 league games for Southampton as well as two FA Cup semi-finals and in one league fixture for Portsmouth before signing for Rovers in December 1932. He was to play in just one league match for Rovers, a 3-1 defeat at Reading, and later worked at a power station.

SATURDAY 4TH SEPTEMBER 1971

One of only five occasions that Rovers have scored five goals before half-time was the convincing 7-1 victory over Bradford City in front of 8,463 spectators at Eastville. Captain Brian Godfrey scored a hat-trick inside the opening 25 minutes, the only one he ever scored for the club, while Harold Jarman and Bobby Jones added two goals each. Colin Hall scored a consolation goal for the Bantams, who fielded Terry Owen, father of the future England striker Michael Owen.

SATURDAY 5TH SEPTEMBER 1925

Ernie Whatmore and Jonah Wilcox both scored as Rovers defeated Gillingham 2-0 at Eastville before a 10,000 crowd in a Third Division (South) fixture. The visiting goalkeeper was Alex Ferguson, whose final league appearance against Rovers was to be for Bristol City in September 1946, just over 21 years later. It is not surprising to hear that no other opponent has a gap of more than 20 years between their first and last league appearances against Rovers.

FRIDAY 6TH SEPTEMBER 1946

Tony Taylor, a full-back who played for Rovers in twelve Second Division games in 1977-78 at the tail-end of a long career, was born in Glasgow. Taylor had played north and south of the border with Morton, Hamilton Academicals, Crystal Palace, Southend United and Swindon Town, but it was from Athlone Town that he joined Rovers in September 1977. Having featured in the disastrous 9-0 hammering at Tottenham Hotspur, he later played for Portsmouth, Kilmarnock, Albion Rovers and Northampton Town. Taylor has since enjoyed three coaching spells in Canada as well as working as youth coach for Celtic.

WEDNESDAY 7TH SEPTEMBER 1932

Such was the impressive form of Rovers' talented centre-forward Viv Gibbins that the club's charismatic manager, Captain Albert Prince-Cox, arranged to fly him from Romford Airport to Filton so that he could feature in a midweek game. Gibbins, an amateur player, was a schoolteacher in the East End of London and could normally play only at weekends. On this occasion, he landed within half an hour of the 6.15pm kick-off and led the line as Rovers recorded a 3-1 victory.

WEDNESDAY 7TH SEPTEMBER 1955

Rovers defeated Liverpool 2-0 at Anfield in Division Two through Geoff Bradford's header three minutes before half-time, from Barrie Meyer's cross. A low shot from Alfie Biggs, cutting in from the right after 59 minutes – on the ground which was to see such undiluted success in the years to come – secured the points. A crowd of 38,320 saw Rovers' only victory to date on this ground.

WEDNESDAY 7TH SEPTEMBER 1960

A poor start to the season was compounded by a 4-0 thumping at Millmoor at the hands of Rotherham United. A crowd of 8,219 saw Keith Kettleborough score twice and Edwin Smith and Alan Kirkman once each for the home side as Rovers fell apart.

MONDAY 7TH SEPTEMBER 1959

Floodlights were used for the first time at Eastville for the 2-1 Second Division victory over Ipswich Town. A crowd of 24,093 saw Peter Hooper score twice for Rovers and Ted Phillips once for the visitors. Although Rovers finished above Ipswich that season, by the summer of 1962 they were in Division Three… while Ipswich were Football League champions.

MONDAY 8TH SEPTEMBER 1930

Howard Radford, who played in goal in 244 league matches for Rovers between 1951 and 1962, was born in Abercynon. Signing from Penrhiwceiber, Radford was a loyal goalkeeper through Rovers' successful years of the 1950s and was instrumental in securing the critical final points to ensure promotion to Division Two. A consistent player, he retired in 1962 to run a succession of pubs in Bristol and Devon and later worked as a security guard.

SUNDAY 8TH SEPTEMBER 1946

Mike Green, who captained Rovers to promotion to Division Two in 1973-74, was born in Carlisle. Formerly with Carlisle United and Gillingham, Green was a central defender who signed for Rovers in July 1971 and played in 74 (plus three as substitute) league matches whilst at Eastville, scoring twice. He later helped Plymouth Argyle to promotion from Division Three and ended his professional career with Torquay United.

SATURDAY 9TH SEPTEMBER 2006

A goalless draw at home to Rochdale gave little indication that Rovers were to gain promotion at the end of the season. A crowd of 4,689 had little to cheer on this occasion at the Memorial Stadium. The Rovers side comprised: Steve Phillips in goal, Ryan Green, Aaron Lescott, Steve Elliott and Craig Hinton in defence; a midfield of James Hunt, Andy Sandell, Sammy Igoe, Craig Disley and Lewis Haldane, with Richard Walker in attack.

MONDAY 10TH SEPTEMBER 1945

'Nobby' Clark scored a hat-trick for Rovers against Aldershot in a wartime Division Three South Southern Section game at Eastville and still ended up on the losing side. Despite the efforts of Clark, which followed an opening goal from Harry Hibbs, Rovers crashed to a 5-4 defeat. Robert Clark appeared for the side in 22 wartime games during the 1945-46 season, contributing 15 goals, but slipped away when professional football was restored in time for the following season.

SATURDAY 11TH SEPTEMBER 1954

The only occasion when all five of the opposition's forward line scored against Rovers in a league fixture was when West Ham United defeated Rovers 5-2 at Upton Park. The match was played in torrential rain and a thunderstorm before a crowd of 22,500. Harry Hooper, Albert Foan, Dave Sexton, John Dick and Jimmy Andrews – numbered consecutively seven to eleven – each scored once in a comfortable victory.

SUNDAY 12TH SEPTEMBER 1954

Jack Lewis, the first Rovers player to win a full international cap whilst with the club, died in Burton-upon-Trent at the age of 72. Born in Aberystwyth in August 1882, Lewis played at inside-right for Wales against England at Cardiff in March 1906. With Rovers as a 17-year-old for the 1899-1900 season, he had left to sign for Portsmouth and Second Division side Burton United before rejoining Rovers in August 1904. During this first season back at Eastville, Rovers were Southern League champions and the outside-left attracted international attention. Having played in 81 Southern League games, in which time he added 30 goals, Lewis moved on to Brighton, Southampton, Croydon Common and Burton United.

SATURDAY 13TH SEPTEMBER 1924

In front of an enthusiastic Eastville crowd of 10,000, Rovers scored three goals in just four minutes midway through the second half of a comfortable 4-0 home victory over Charlton Athletic in Division Three (South). Ernie Whatmore had already put Rovers ahead, before three quick goals secured an easy victory. Whatmore completed his hat-trick and young forward Syd Holcroft scored for the fifth league match in succession. A popular, bald-headed leader of the line, Whatmore contributed 40 goals in 134 league appearances for Rovers before joining Queens Park Rangers in 1928.

WEDNESDAY 14TH SEPTEMBER 1960

Martin Shaw, a midfielder who played for Rovers in the 1978-79 season, was born in Bristol. Just 18 when he came on as substitute for David Williams in the 1-0 defeat at home to Preston in May 1979, Shaw started the following game, a 1-0 victory at Wrexham. This proved the extent of his league career, though, for Shaw joined Bath City that summer and played 56 (plus two as substitute) times for the Twerton Park club over two seasons, scoring three times, before joining Forest Green Rovers and Banbury.

WEDNESDAY 15TH SEPTEMBER 1954

Rovers scored three times at Anfield, only for John Evans to score all Liverpool's goals in their 5-3 win. It was a devastating show of goalscoring from an underrated forward and his achievement remains a Liverpool record equalled only by Andy McGuigan and Ian Rush; only Blackburn's Tommy Briggs and Luton's Joe Payne have scored more against Rovers in an individual match. The prolific Peter Hooper scored twice for Rovers and full-back Harry Bamford once before a crowd of 31,100.

SATURDAY 15TH SEPTEMBER 1956

When Rovers were awarded penalties in the 1950s, the crowd always anticipated Peter Hooper delivering one of his pile-drivers. When Leicester City visited Eastville, Hooper took a penalty with his usual venomous shot, but the ball struck a post and rebounded with such ferocity that Leicester broke away and scored. Rovers lost 2-1. A crowd of 28,500 saw popular forward Barrie Meyer score for Rovers, while Arthur Rowley and Tommy McDonald scored for Leicester.

PETER HOOPER POWERFUL PENALTY CREATED AN OPPOSITION GOAL IN SEPTEMBER 1956

THURSDAY 16TH SEPTEMBER 1999

Bill Dodgin, who represented Rovers as a player and as a manager, died in a nursing home in Godalming, aged 90. Born in April 1909 in Gateshead, Dodgin had played for Huddersfield Town, Lincoln City and Charlton Athletic, before joining Rovers as a wing-half in May 1936. He played in 30 league games for Rovers, scoring once, before appearing for Orient and Southampton and managing Fulham, Brentford and Sampdoria. Dodgin, who was Rovers' manager from November 1969 to July 1972, started to assemble the side that gained promotion to Division Two in 1973-74.

SATURDAY 17TH SEPTEMBER 1949

An unchanged Rovers side drew 0-0 with Bournemouth in front of a crowd of 18,548 at Eastville in Division Three (South). Jack Weare was in goal, with Harry Bamford and Geoff Fox a popular full-back pairing; three half-backs in Jackie Pitt, veteran Ray Warren and Frank McCourt; Bryan Bush, Len Hodges, Bill Roost, Tony James and Josser Watling were in the forward line.

WEDNESDAY 18TH SEPTEMBER 1918

Phil Taylor, whose first-half hat-trick as an 18-year-old for Rovers in a cup tie against Oldham Athletic set him on the road to stardom, was born in Bristol. A wing-half and inside-forward, Taylor added two goals in his 21 league appearances for Rovers before a high-profile move to Liverpool in March 1936. He was to appear in over 300 league games either side of the war for the Anfield side, winning a league championship medal and captaining the Reds to victory in the 1950 FA Cup final, as well as winning three England caps. Latterly manager at Liverpool, Taylor is believed to be, at the time of going to print, the oldest living Rovers player.

SATURDAY 19TH SEPTEMBER 1896

Rovers' Western League season opened with a 1-0 defeat before a 4,000 crowd at home to Bedminster at Ridgeway, George Cottle scoring before half-time. Rovers fielded Bill Stone in goal; Frank Marriott and Bill Nolan at full-back; club captain Hugh McBain, Novello Shenton and George Hockin in the half-back line and five forwards in Bill Thompson, Richard Osborne, Fred Gallier, George Brown and Ernie Harvey.

SATURDAY 20TH SEPTEMBER 2003

The first time a Rovers substitute was sent off was when Simon Bryant received a red card for a two-footed tackle on York City's player-manager Chris Brass, just six minutes after coming on to the field at Bootham Crescent. Rovers lost the Third Division fixture 2-1, with Junior Agogo and York's Lee Bullock and Aaron Wilford having scored first-half goals before a crowd of 3,968. The only other Rovers substitute, to date, to receive a red card was Richard Walker in the single-goal defeat at Swindon in November 2007.

SUNDAY 21ST SEPTEMBER 1879

Harry Wassell, who played 13 times for Rovers in their 1904-05 Southern League championship campaign, was born in Stourbridge. Having signed for Small Heath, now Birmingham City, from Brierley Hill Alliance in 1901, he played in 56 league matches as a left-back before arriving at Eastville in May 1904. Twelve months later he joined Queens Park Rangers, the third and final game he played for them being their 7-0 drubbing of Rovers. A solid defender and strong team man, Wassell died in Dudley in March 1951.

SATURDAY 22ND SEPTEMBER 1894

The first ever meeting of the clubs destined to be Bristol Rovers and Bristol City took place at St John's Lane, Bedminster in a 4.40pm kick-off – delayed by a lifeboat demonstration – as Bristol South End defeated Eastville Rovers 2-1. Rovers, captained by Claude Hodgson, were grateful to centre-forward Bob Horsey for his goal, after Rovers had trailed 2-0 at half-time. Two 20-year-olds on the verge of great careers, Hamlet Horatio Clements and Frank Ernest Mayger, scored South End's goals.

SATURDAY 23RD SEPTEMBER 1995

Two Brentford players, Martin Grainger and Jamie Bates, were sent off during Rovers' comfortable 2-0 league win at Twerton Park. This was the third of eight occasions when Rovers' opponents have received at least two red cards in a league game. Rovers scored a goal in each half in front of a crowd of 5,131, with Marcus Stewart's first-half penalty preceding midfielder Martin Paul's late goal. In the return fixture at Griffin Park, Rovers were to grind out a goalless draw.

SATURDAY 24th SEPTEMBER 1921

What was to become Rovers' home was opened and named the Memorial Ground by G B Britton, Lord Mayor of Bristol. The land had been purchased for £26,000 and developed from wartime allotments on the evocatively-named Buffalo Bill's Field. This new ground was dedicated to the memory of the 300 rugby players from Bristol who had lost their lives in World War I. Two local roads commemorate Harry Willoughby Beloe, the rugby club's president at that time.

WEDNESDAY 25th SEPTEMBER 1929

During the inter-war years, Rovers often travelled to away matches by charabanc. On the way to Brentford, their vehicle hit an electric standard and three windows were smashed. Fortunately, no one was injured and the team continued on the way to Griffin Park. Rovers led through a Jack Phillips goal and Cyril Blakemore, the Bees' summer signing from Bristol City, missed a penalty. Brentford, though, scored twice in the last few minutes to win 2-1, their second goal coming direct from a corner from Jackie Forster, and went on to win all 21 home league fixtures that season.

SATURDAY 26th SEPTEMBER 1925

Prior to the kick-off of Rovers' 1-0 defeat at Luton Town, the Bishop of St. Albans gave an address to the 7,000 crowd as part of Luton Mission Week. Rovers lost to a second-half goal from Welsh-born forward Syd Reid. The bishop, Rt. Rev. Michael Furse, had been Archdeacon of Johannesburg from 1903 to 1909 and had then spent eleven years as Bishop of Pretoria before moving to St. Albans in 1920.

MONDAY 26th SEPTEMBER 1960

The first team to win a League Cup tie was Rovers. The first round of the inaugural tournament was due to take place 24 hours later, but the Rovers against Fulham game at Eastville was brought forward. A crowd of 20,022 saw Maurice Cook give Fulham an early lead, the first goal scored by any player in this tournament, only for goals from Harold Jarman and the evergreen Geoff Bradford to earn Rovers a 2-1 victory. Rovers then defeated Reading in round two before being eliminated by Rotherham United.

SATURDAY 27TH SEPTEMBER 1997

Three goals down after 25 minutes, Rovers were level by half-time in an astonishing 4-4 draw before a crowd of 5,990 at Oldham Athletic's Boundary Park. Stuart Barlow had scored twice and Sean McCarthy once early on for Oldham, only for Rovers to reply through two goals from Peter Beadle and one from Barry Hayles. Shaun Garnett gave Oldham the lead again after an hour, only for Rovers to claim a point through Jamie Cureton's penalty three minutes from time.

WEDNESDAY 27TH SEPTEMBER 2000

A crowd of over 25,000 at Goodison Park, which included over three thousand from Bristol, had seen Premiership Everton – who fielded the veteran England midfielder Paul Gascoigne as a substitute – stunned by Lewis Hogg's volleyed equaliser three minutes from time in a Worthington Cup tie. Then, on an emotional night of high drama at the Memorial Stadium, Marcus Bignot's 58th-minute goal, after Nathan Ellington's initial shot had been saved, took Rovers into a penalty shoot-out where Dwayne Plummer successfully converted the decisive kick to give the home side a 4-2 penalty victory and a memorable scalp.

SATURDAY 28TH SEPTEMBER 1935

Trailing 3-0 at half-time away to Northampton Town, Rovers staged a dramatic recovery to earn an unlikely draw. Before a crowd of 7,102, Tommy Bell, Ron Hinson and Len Potter had given the Potters an apparently unassailable lead, only for Rovers to score three times in the final 20 minutes to draw 3-3. Forward Eli Postin, who was making his only league appearance of the season, Vince Harwood and Jack Woodman were Rovers' scorers in a remarkable comeback.

SATURDAY 29TH SEPTEMBER 2007

The seventh and most recent occasion that a Rovers player has scored two penalties in a league fixture was when Richard Walker's two spot kicks gave Rovers a comfortable lead at home to Leyton Orient. Two goals ahead after 54 minutes, Rovers took their foot off the pedal and the despairing home crowd of 7,181 was left still searching for the first home win of the season after goals from Wayne Gray, Tamika Mkandawire and Jason Demetriou earned Orient a 3-2 victory.

SATURDAY 30TH SEPTEMBER 1905

Rovers set about defending the Southern League championship of 1904-05 with a run of four wins and a draw in their opening five games, the final match of this sequence being a 2-1 home victory over Millwall before an Eastville crowd of 10,000. Rovers were deprived the luxury of fielding an unchanged side, when outside-left Albert Dunkley pulled out injured and his place was taken by Scotsman John Haxton. Goals from Billy Clark and Jack Lewis earned Rovers victory, with Millwall's Welsh international Dick Jones scoring to make the half-time score 1-1. The excellent start to the season, though, could not be maintained and, losing 7-1 at Luton Town in their very next fixture, Rovers finished the campaign in eighth place in the table.

SUNDAY 30TH SEPTEMBER 1956

Trevor Morgan, who scored 24 goals in 54 (plus one as substitute) league matches as a striker for Rovers in the 1980s, was born in Forest Gate, London. Formerly with Bournemouth, Mansfield Town, Bristol City and Exeter City, Morgan could boast a wealth of experience and a hat-trick against Rotherham United just weeks after joining the club in the autumn of 1985 sealed his popularity with the fans. Rejoining Bristol City for £16,000 in January 1987, Morgan also played for Bolton Wanderers and Colchester United. He coached in Hong Kong and Australia, settling on the north coast of Lake Macquarie.

SATURDAY 30TH SEPTEMBER 2006

Rovers slumped to their sixth defeat of the league season and dropped to 19th place in League Two after a 2-0 defeat at Chester City. James Walker's full debut in attack, at the expense of Lewis Haldane, left Rovers with the 'Walker Brothers', Richard and James, in attack. Mid-table Chester had only scored eleven times in their first eleven games, but first-half goals from Kevin Sandwith, after 18 minutes, and Roberto Martinez 20 minutes later, earned the home side a comfortable victory. Incredibly, though, some eight months later, Rovers were promoted to League One.

BRISTOL ROVERS
On This Day

OCTOBER

SATURDAY 1st OCTOBER 1892

For the club's first-ever Bristol and District League match, Rovers were due to play at home but had to give up ground advantage and lost 3-1 to Mangotsfield United in a 3.30pm kick-off. Bill Nolan scored the first for the opposition after 15 minutes and Courtney Punter added two in the second half, one a penalty. Walter Perrin's late goal was all Rovers had to show for their efforts.

SATURDAY 1st OCTOBER 1949

Before a frustrated home crowd of 14,906, Rovers lost 2-0 at Eastville at the hands of Watford in a Third Division (South) fixture. Veteran Welsh forward Dave Thomas scored both goals.

WEDNESDAY 1st OCTOBER 1969

Sandy Allan, later a Rovers player, scored a hat-trick of headers as Cardiff City defeated Mjoendalen 5-1 in a European Cup Winners' Cup tie en route to registering a 12-2 aggregate victory. The only other player with Rovers connections to score a hat-trick in European cup tournaments was Alan Ball, who scored three times in Everton's 6-2 European Cup win over Keflavik of Iceland in 1970 and was to play for Rovers just over a decade later.

SATURDAY 2nd OCTOBER 1954

The visit of Swansea Town to Eastville attracted a crowd of 28,731. Mel Charles, having scored in both fixtures against Rovers the previous season, put through his own net after only six minutes and Geoff Bradford doubled Rovers' lead nine minutes later. After half-time, Bradford scored again after 55 minutes, Peter Hooper scored on the hour mark, Ron Burgess contributed an own goal twelve minutes later and Bill Roost added a sixth with a quarter of an hour left. Hooper's second goal, in the last minute, meant Rovers had equalled the club record 7-0 league victory. Rovers later defeated Shrewsbury Town 7-0 in March 1964. It was also the second of only three occasions that the opposition has contributed two own goals in a league match.One footnote is that Ron Burgess's own goal marks him down as the oldest opponent to have conceded an own goal in Rovers' favour in the Football League; he was 37 years 176 days.

SUNDAY 2ND OCTOBER 1955

Only one player has represented England whilst on Bristol Rovers' books. Geoff Bradford played in the forward line in Copenhagen as England recorded a 5-1 victory. Characteristically, he scored the fifth himself, with a low right-foot shot eight minutes from time, following Jackie Milburn's flighted cross pass. This was to be Bradford's only England cap. Rovers' Supporters' Club chartered an aeroplane to fly from Whitchurch Airport to Copenhagen, with 34 on board including his proud mother as guest of honour.

SATURDAY 2ND OCTOBER 1965

With substitutes having been permitted in league matches from the start of the 1965-66 season it took until the ninth game of the campaign for Rovers to use their twelfth man. For the home game against Walsall, Joe Davis became the first Rovers substitute to join the action late on, as Rovers recorded a comfortable 3-0 home win; Harold Jarman and Bobby Jones (two) scoring before an Eastville crowd of 9,357.

TUESDAY 3RD OCTOBER 1916

Joe Hulme was killed in action, one of three Rovers players who were to die in the First World War. Born in Leek in December 1877, he had played for Rovers in four Southern League games in the 1901-02 season before furthering his career at Brighton & Hove Albion. Walter Gerrish and John Hardman were the other two former Rovers players who were killed in the Great War of 1914-18; numerous professional footballers from many countries lost their lives during the conflict.

SATURDAY 3RD OCTOBER 1925

Joe Walter, who played for Rovers in two spells in the 1920s, found his 'goal' disallowed because two sheep had wandered on to the pitch and the referee had blown his whistle to hold up play. Walter was playing for Taunton Town in their FA Cup tie with Torquay United which was lost 2-1. Born in August 1895, he had played for Rovers between 1920 and 1922 and later returned to Eastville in the 1928-29 season, scoring 19 times in 164 league matches for Rovers. He also won a league championship medal with Huddersfield Town in 1923-24. Joe Walter died in May 1995, aged 99.

SATURDAY 3rd OCTOBER 1931

As Rovers struggled to get back into a game at home to Norwich City – where they trailed to a Cyril Blakemore goal – a late appeal for a penalty was turned down. At the final whistle, a spectator got onto the pitch and attempted to assault the referee, future FIFA President, S. F. Rous. On the same day in 1928, Rovers reserves had played Plymouth Argyle reserves, whose centre-half Jack Pullen punched referee A. J. Attwood twice after being sent off.

SATURDAY 4th OCTOBER 1947

A second consecutive home league match was lost, as Northampton Town, before an Eastville crowd of 15,098, won by two goals to one. Dynamic forward Fred Leamon was Rovers' goalscorer, whilst the Cobblers' top scorer Jimmy Briscoe scored their opening goal. Veteran Alf Morrall also scored.

SATURDAY 5th OCTOBER 1895

Warmley defeated Rovers 2-0, in the Eastville club's first-ever FA Cup tie. There was a crowd of 1,500 at Rudgway, Rovers' home ground for this fixture. Rovers, who had defeated Warmley 2-1 only two weeks earlier, lined up with: Louis Johns in goal; Bob Horsey and Fred Lovett at full-back; a half-back line of captain Hugh McBain, Claude Hodgson and George Hockin; and five forwards in Archie Laurie, George Brown, Fred Gallier, Bill Thompson and Charlie Leese. This first foray into the FA Cup led to disappointment, as Rovers lost 2-0, with 'Nipper' Britton and Bill Bowler, from a classic header, scoring in the space of two first-half minutes on a rain-soaked pitch.

WEDNESDAY 6th OCTOBER 1948

Larry Lloyd, a Bristol-born central defender who played 43 times in the league for Rovers, scoring once, in the 1968-69 season, was born. A record sale of £55,000 in April 1969 took the young player to Liverpool and he later played for Coventry City, Nottingham Forest and Wigan Athletic, winning two European Cup medals at Forest, league championship medals at both Liverpool and Forest, as well as playing in FA Cup, League Cup and UEFA Cup finals. He also won four full England caps before retiring to become manager at Wigan Athletic and later Notts County.

FRIDAY 6TH OCTOBER 1950

David Staniforth, a bearded striker who scored 32 league goals for Rovers in 135 (plus 16 as substitute) matches between 1974 and 1979, was born in Chesterfield. Formerly at Sheffield United, Staniforth joined Rovers in a £20,000 deal in March 1974 in time to make an impact in Rovers' Second Division campaigns. After leaving Eastville, he represented both Bradford City and Halifax Town.

SATURDAY 7TH OCTOBER 1922

A fourth league win of the season was secured as goals from Fred Lunn and Sam Furniss helped defeat Southend United 2-0 at Eastville, before a 9,000 crowd. Rovers had made one change to their side, recalling the experienced Jock Rutherford in place of right-half Harry Boxley. Incredibly, Rovers were to embark on a run of 560 minutes without a goal following Furniss's 75th-minute strike, a club record that remained until 2001.

FRIDAY 7TH OCTOBER 1977

Bert Densley, who had given Rovers sterling service in the 1920s, had a leg amputated at Bristol Royal Infirmary; he was to lose the other one later. Densley, a locally-born goalkeeper, had played in 23 league matches for Rovers, though he was on the books from February 1924 until August 1931, largely serving as understudy to Jesse Whatley. By 1977 Bert Densley was living in Newbury Road, Horfield and he died in Bristol in June 1982.

SATURDAY 8TH OCTOBER 1887

Edward Tucker, Rovers' normally reliable goalkeeper, was forced to miss the entire second half of the game at St. George through injury. Rovers, who led 2-1 at the interval of a match that had unusually kicked off at 3.40pm, managed to hold on with ten men for a 3-2 victory. Inside-forward Fred Griffiths scored twice and the winning goal was scored by Bill Perrin. Two Perrin brothers played for Rovers around this time, Bill being the youngest of five children to Edward Perrin, a Bristolian boilermaker, and his wife Martha, who had been born at the Cape of Good Hope. Bill Perrin played for Rovers on 40 occasions between 1885 and 1891, scoring 15 goals; he died in Exmoor in the autumn of 1941.

SATURDAY 8TH OCTOBER 1910

Having lost the first six games of the season, scoring just once in the process, Rovers defeated Plymouth Argyle 2-1 to kick-start their season. A 5,000 crowd at Home Park saw Billy Peplow and Frank Woodhall, with his only strike in Rovers' colours, score for Rovers, with Bill Baker replying for Argyle.

WEDNESDAY 9TH OCTOBER 1991

Having lost 3-1 at home to Bristol City in a League Cup first leg, few gave Rovers any chance of success. However, inspired by a large and vociferous travelling band of supporters, Rovers pulled out all the stops to win 5-4 on aggregate. At Ashton Gate, a crowd of 9,880 saw Rovers score three times in a strong second-half display as they won 4-2 to defeat their local rivals on the away goals rule. On a night of typically high passions, old heads Devon White and David Mehew scored twice each.

SATURDAY 9TH OCTOBER 1993

In an astonishing climax to the game, Rovers came from behind to defeat Bradford City 4-3 at Twerton Park, thanks to two very late penalties from Marcus Stewart. This was the sixth of only seven occasions that a Rovers player has converted two penalties in the same league fixture. There was a crowd of 5,323 in Bath for the game and Paul Showler's first-ever league goal gave the Bantams a half-time lead. Rovers scored four second-half goals to claim an exciting victory – with John Taylor and Worrell Sterling also scoring – whilst Lee Duxbury added two more for the visitors.

TUESDAY 9TH OCTOBER 2007

Having reached the final the previous season, Rovers slipped anonymously out of the Johnstone's Paint Trophy, losing 1-0 to struggling AFC Bournemouth. Jo Kuffour, who joined Rovers a year later, scored the only goal in front of 3,313 spectators at the Memorial Stadium. The visitors were even able, in an injury crisis, to bring on the veteran Rob Newman as a late substitute, just over 25 years after he had first played against Rovers in the colours of Bristol City. Born in December 1963, he was just short of his 44 birthday.

SATURDAY 10TH OCTOBER 1998

In losing 3-1 in front of a crowd of 6,023 at Northampton Town, Rovers were reduced to nine men, as goalscorer Michael Meaker, after 68 minutes, and Trevor Challis in the final seconds, were both shown red cards. Bizarrely, this was the second time in a week that two Rovers players had been sent off in the same league fixture. Seven days earlier, Jason Roberts had been shown the red card after 60 minutes, and Rob Trees after 70, as nine-man Rovers defeated AFC Bournemouth 1-0 at The Memorial Stadium.

SATURDAY 11TH OCTOBER 1890

Despite leading by two goals at half-time, Rovers were defeated 4-2 at Bedminster in front of an 'enthusiastic' crowd in a Bristol and District League match. Rovers lined up: Edward Tucker in goal; a full-back pairing of Bill Somerton and Claude Hodgson; Bill Wallace, Bill Brown and Fred Lovett in the half-back line; and a forward line of brothers Archie and Frank Laurie, Fred Yates, Fred Channing and Bill Perrin. The last-name, a 23-year-old local forward, scored both Rovers' goals and netted 15 times in his 40 games for the Eastville club.

WEDNESDAY 11TH OCTOBER 1972

Rovers faced a team including nine full internationals in a League Cup replay against Manchester United in front of an Old Trafford crowd of 29,349 and the veteran winger Bobby Jones was recalled to add experience to the Third Division side. After Dick Sheppard had saved well from Bobby Charlton, John Rudge put Rovers ahead after 30 minutes when he headed home a corner taken by Lindsay Parsons. Midway through the second half the home side was awarded a controversial penalty when Ian Storey-Moore fell under a challenge from Frankie Prince. Sheppard saved George Best's kick. Good fortune could not last forever, though, and substitute Sammy McIlroy headed home an equaliser from a Willie Morgan corner with ten minutes left. Sensationally, four minutes later – a third header from a corner – Bruce Bannister's goal created by Kenny Stephens gave Rovers one of the greatest victories in the club's history. The 2-1 win is the only occasion Rovers have won a competitive fixture at Old Trafford; the only league encounter on this ground was a 2-0 defeat in September 1974.

SATURDAY 12TH OCTOBER 1889

Rovers led 2-0 at half-time, though none of their players had yet scored. The hosts, Warmley, were overly generous early on, conceding two own goals: the first, through Gay after 15 minutes and then through Wilmot who netted 20 minutes later. After the interval, Warmley came back into the game more and, with the prolific Walter Perrin adding Rovers' third goal after 75 minutes, the sides shared a 3-3 draw.

SATURDAY 12TH OCTOBER 1946

When central defender Ray Warren scored from the penalty spot against Queens Park Rangers in a Third Division (South) fixture, it was just a few days short of ten years since he had last registered a league strike for Rovers. Obviously, war had claimed many of those years, but the nine years and eleven months since he scored against Walsall in November 1936 remains the longest gap between league goals for Rovers by any player. Sam Irving, a future Rovers wing-half, had gone over twelve years without a goal from scoring for Bristol City in October 1914, to adding another for Cardiff City in March 1927.

MONDAY 13TH OCTOBER 1947

A legendary figure in long shorts, striking a heavy, brown ball, Arthur Ormston died in Oldham at the early age of 47. Born in Alnwick, Northumberland in June 1900, Ormston played for eight lower league clubs, scoring eight goals in his first two appearances for Oldham Athletic and scored freely wherever he went. He arrived at Eastville in June 1927 in a £300 deal from Bradford City and scored 15 times in 27 league matches before returning for a second spell at Oldham.

SATURDAY 14TH OCTOBER 1893

As football became an increasingly central part of working men's lives, there was greater demand for up-to-date information for an ever more literate readership. The Reform Act of 1884 had led to prominent politicians taking a greater interest in football as a means of wooing voters and the recent introduction of half-days on Saturdays allowed attendances at local sports matches to be boosted. On this day in 1893, the *Bristol Evening News* brought out its first Special Saturday Football Edition.

SATURDAY 15TH OCTOBER 1977

Having signed a big-name player in Bobby Gould, the Rovers management hoped they would not be disappointed. By half-time on his club debut, Gould had already scored a hat-trick – after three, 13 and 35 minutes – and the transfer fee was already justified. Before an Eastville crowd of 6,431, Rovers defeated Blackburn Rovers 4-1 at Eastville, with David Staniforth also scoring for Rovers after half-time and Noel Brotherston replying for the visitors. A much-travelled striker, Gould was to score twelve times in almost 40 league outings with Rovers. He later returned to the club as manager in two spells, between 1981 and 1983 and from 1985 to 1987.

WEDNESDAY 16TH OCTOBER 1844

Rovers' history is intertwined with stories of water and flooding. The ground at Eastville had a long-running battle with the River Frome next door and the lyrics of Goodnight Irene reflect this struggle. However, this theme precedes Rovers' foundation. Love-struck 28-year-old Hester Tilly, much in the character of Shakespeare's Ophelia, threw herself into a pond in her parents' orchard approximately where Muller Road stands today, after her secret illicit affair with a farmhand named Williams was uncovered. She drowned and was buried by torchlight just before midnight that night, as was the tradition in cases of suicide at that time.

SATURDAY 16TH OCTOBER 1971

York City's John Mackin became only the fifth opponent to convert two penalties in a league fixture with Rovers. A crowd of 6,876 witnessed an extraordinary game which featured six goals before half-time. Kenny Stephens and Harold Jarman put Rovers 2-0 up in nine minutes and Jarman's second fired Rovers 3-1 ahead. But Mackin's first penalty, awarded on the stroke of half-time for a foul by Lindsay Parsons, left the scores level at the break. Stephens put Rovers ahead again after 57 minutes and, four minutes later Jarman completed the second hat-trick of his Rovers career to put the Pirates 5-3 ahead. Rovers held on for a 5-4 victory, despite a second Mackin penalty after handball against Bobby Brown – in his penultimate start before a transfer to Weymouth – 18 minutes from time.

SATURDAY 17TH OCTOBER 1953

When Birmingham City came to Eastville for a Second Division fixture, this attracted the highest crowd Rovers have ever drawn for a home game in the Football League. There were 35,614 crammed into the old stadium at Eastville to witness an exciting 1-1 draw. Geoff Bradford scored Rovers' goal past the England goalkeeper Gil Merrick and Ted Purdon, a Rovers player later in his career, scored for Birmingham.

SUNDAY 18TH OCTOBER 1998

The former Rovers goalkeeper Dick Sheppard died in Bristol at the age of 53. An enormously popular player, he was born in Bristol in February 1945 and made 151 league appearances for Rovers between 1969 and 1974, and also played for West Bromwich Albion, whom he represented in the 1967 League Cup final, and Torquay United. He was seriously injured during his 150th league game for Rovers against Tranmere Rovers at Eastville in January 1973 when he suffered a depressed fracture of the skull. Sheppard returned to the side for one final game almost two years later.

SUNDAY 19TH OCTOBER 1980

The day after Rovers' dramatic 3-3 draw at home to Sheffield Wednesday, central defender Mike Trought was born in Bristol. A trainee with the club, Trought made his league bow at Maine Road before a crowd of 24,976 as Rovers drew 2-2 in their first-ever league encounter with Manchester City. Briefly in the Welsh under-21 squad, he was to play in eight (plus five more as substitute) league fixtures with the Gas. In July 2002, beset with injury problems, he joined Bath City, captaining his side in a friendly that summer against Rovers, and he later appeared for Clevedon Town and Paulton Rovers.

SATURDAY 19TH OCTOBER 1996

Both Rovers and Bristol Rugby Club played home games on the Memorial Ground pitch in quick succession. In a 3pm kick-off, Rovers played out a goalless draw in Division Two against Blackpool, a game watched by 5,823 people. Bristol then kicked off against Narbonne in a European Conference Group B game that started at 7.30pm; a crowd of 2,000 saw the French visitors win 18-16.

TUESDAY 19TH OCTOBER 2004

The most unlikely of draws was the product of a tempestuous home local derby with Yeovil Town, watched by 9,295 fans. After dominating early play, Rovers had fallen behind to a deflected Paul Terry goal. In injury time at the end of the first half, the visitors' Gavin Williams crashed to the floor and Rovers' Dave Savage, who had clearly lashed out, though without making contact, was sent off by referee Phil Crossley. Within a minute, Steve Elliott became the second Rovers player to be dismissed as the atmosphere turned sour. Swiftly 2-0 down, nine-man Rovers then staged a comeback of epic proportions, as first James Hunt and then, with four minutes remaining, man-of-the-match Junior Agogo completed Rovers' unexpected yet, on the basis of their second-half display, well-merited recovery.

WEDNESDAY 20TH OCTOBER 1948

Wayne Jones – a hugely talented Rovers inside-forward who won one full cap for Wales against Finland in 1971 – was born in Treorchy. Joining Rovers initially as an amateur, Jones made his debut for the club as a teenager and, between February 1967 and November 1972, he scored 28 goals in 218 (plus six as substitute) league matches before a knee injury forced his premature retirement at the age of 24. Later, he worked in the Middle East and was physiotherapist at Shrewsbury Town, Huddersfield Town and Notts County.

SATURDAY 21ST OCTOBER 1933

In a feat unlikely ever to be repeated for any Rovers side, George Tadman scored twice direct from corners during Rovers reserves' 6-2 win against Torquay United reserves at Eastville. Tom Cowan and George Berry scored two rather more conventional goals each in this game. A 19-year-old outside-right from Kent, Tadman was to play five times in the league for Rovers between 1933 and 1935, scoring twice; once against Gillingham, and once against Charlton Athletic. He became player-manager at Street and coached in France before taking on coaching duties with Rovers in the 1950s. A brother of Maurice Tadman, the former Charlton Athletic and Plymouth Argyle player, George died in Bristol in September 1994 at the age of 80.

SATURDAY 22ND OCTOBER 1977

Tottenham Hotspur's relegation to Division Two meant a first-ever league meeting with Rovers and television cameras were there to record the game before a crowd of 26,311 at White Hart Lane. It turned into a living nightmare for Rovers, who crashed to their heaviest post-war defeat. For all the pre-match optimism Rovers, three goals behind by half-time, with the former Bristol City striker Colin Lee opening the scoring after five minutes, conceded four goals in a nine-minute spell and ended up being beaten 9-0. Lee scored four goals on his Spurs debut and Ian Moores added three in 26 second-half minutes, only the third occasion two opponents had scored hat-tricks in a league game against Rovers. Future England international managers scored in the last minute of each half; Peter Taylor on the stroke of half-time and Glenn Hoddle the soul-destroying ninth in the dying seconds. One player singled out for praise was 18-year-old goalkeeper Glyn Jones, who was largely credited with keeping the score down to single figures. He played on the same pitch nine days later, helping the reserves to a 1-1 draw.

THURSDAY 23RD OCTOBER 1947

Following allegations of the misappropriation of club funds, Rovers' club secretary Charles Ferrari was forced to resign. He was replaced by John Gummow, who was joined from 1949 by an additional secretary in Ron Moules, who held down a position with the club until 1967. Ferrari had been appointed secretary on August 20th 1945, when Con Stevens, who had the majority of shares in the greyhound company that had just bought Eastville Stadium, had taken over as Rovers' chairman.

SATURDAY 24TH OCTOBER 1964

The only Rovers player to score a league hat-trick and end up on the losing side is Ian Hamilton, whose three goals could not prevent Rovers from being defeated 6-3 by Southend United at Roots Hall. This fate has befallen four opponents: Liverpool's Kevin Lewis in 1961, Northampton Town's Frank Large in 1967, Ian Wood of Oldham the following year and Brentford's Denny Mundee in 1994. On this occasion, though, a crowd of 6,343 at Roots Hall saw Southend, 4-1 up by half-time, win through goals from John McKinven (3), Ray Smith (2) and Andy Smillie.

WEDNESDAY 24TH OCTOBER 1979

There were 4,000 people at Eastville Stadium to watch Rovers take on the touring Zambian national side in a novelty friendly, which Rovers won 4-1. Paul Randall, on-loan Phil Lythgoe, Miah Dennehy and David Williams scored for the home side. Having already defeated Holland 3-2 in November 1930, Rovers could now lay claim to having won matches against two full international sides.

WEDNESDAY 24TH OCTOBER 1990

A New Zealand international defender, Ceri Evans, was sent off against Rovers in the victory over Oxford United, Rovers' third successive league win. This match at Twerton Park, before a crowd of 5,526, was won 1-0 by Rovers through a penalty from midfield talisman Ian Holloway. Evans, who played for Oxford United from 1989 to 1993, won 56 full caps for New Zealand, scoring two international goals.

WEDNESDAY 25TH OCTOBER 1882

The flood waters that play such a critical role in Rovers' history claimed a life in Mina Road. The Baptist Mills and Eastville areas were badly affected by rising water and the stock of the Black Swan on Stapleton Road was under five feet of water. Nineteen-year-old Fred Foot, attempting to deliver bread from Williams' bakery of Easton, was swept away along with his pony, from beside the railway bridge in Mina Road. Despite rescue attempts made by three locals and a policeman, both deliveryman and pony were drowned. This tragic incident was one of several in late Victorian times as East Bristol fought a perennial struggle against rising flood water.

THURSDAY 25TH OCTOBER 1956

Wayne Powell – who scored a hat-trick when Rovers defeated Sheffield United 3-1 at Eastville in May 1977, completing his haul with an 88th minute header from a deep right-wing cross at the Muller Road End – was born in Caerphilly. Initially an apprentice at the club, Powell scored on his debut as an 18-year-old substitute and went on to contribute ten goals in 25 (plus seven as substitute) league matches before representing Halifax Town and Hereford United in Division Four. His son Lewis was on Rovers' books in the early years of the 21st century.

SATURDAY 25TH OCTOBER 2008

It was the Rickie Lambert show at the Memorial Stadium as the top goalscorer in all four divisions scored four times to equal a club individual record and demolish high-flying Southend United before a crowd of 7,055. Lambert scored after ten, 16, 33 and 55 minutes, before a mini-revival from Southend saw both Peter Clarke and substitute Francis Laurent score late on to make the final score 4-2. The prolific scorer contributed 29 of Rovers' 79 league goals that season.

WEDNESDAY 26TH OCTOBER 1955

Phil Bater, who played as a full-back in 301 (plus nine as substitute) league matches for Rovers, scoring three times, was born in Cardiff. An apprentice with Rovers, Bater signed professional forms in October 1973 and played regularly in two spells, either side of a couple of seasons with Wrexham, before leaving Rovers for Brentford in 1986. He joined Cardiff City a year later and was sent off on his club debut, before returning to Bristol to work as a landscape gardener.

MONDAY 27TH OCTOBER 1997

For many years, the greyhound track around the Eastville pitch was not just an iconic image but also a symbol of the fact that finances were tight for Rovers. The club had sold the ground to the greyhound company in 1940 to raise the £12,000 that was deemed to be critical at that time to the club's survival. The last greyhound race at Eastville in 1997 saw entry fees sentimentally waived and this signalled the end of the road for the stadium, with the Swedish furniture giants IKEA arriving on the site 18 months later.

WEDNESDAY 28TH OCTOBER 1914

John Hardman, who was killed in France in February 1917 whilst serving as an army sergeant, joined Rovers from Derby County. Born in Miles Platting in Lancashire in 1889, the oldest child of John and Sarah Hardman, he was to play 23 times for Rovers as a wing-half before the onset of war ended his professional career. Joe Hulme and Walter Gerrish were the two other former Rovers players who lost their lives in action during World War I.

SATURDAY 28TH OCTOBER 1967

A most remarkable victory came at Northampton Town in front of a crowd of 9,126. Ray Mabbutt scored a hat-trick; there were six first-half goals, a hat-trick scorer for each club for the second and most recent time in Rovers' club history, and an astonishing 5-4 win for the Pirates. In the first half the Cobblers led twice and Rovers once, with home centre-forward Frank Large scoring twice and winning the penalty converted by John Mackin, who scored two penalties when York City visited Eastville in October 1971. Mabbutt had scored when Johnny Williams had his shot parried, while Bobby Jones, against his former club, and Williams, had also found the net. Level 3-3 at half-time, Rovers took the lead again through Mabbutt and, after Large scored his third of the game, so too did Mabbutt to record the only hat-trick of his career and give Rovers an unlikely 5-4 win.

SATURDAY 28TH OCTOBER 1995

Following a change in league regulations, it was now permissible to use three substitutes in a league game. The first occasion that Rovers used as many as three in one game was at Brighton & Hove Albion, where Ian McLean, Martin Paul and Tom White replaced Ian Wright, Mike Davis and Justin Channing. Rovers lost the game 2-0 before a crowd of 5,658, the opening goal after 51 minutes being a freak affair. In truth, goalkeeper Andy Collett had not seen Brighton's George Parris waiting by the goalpost as he shaped to take a goal-kick. When Collett grounded the ball, Parris tackled him, rounded him and scored in the empty net to set up a comfortable win.

WEDNESDAY 29TH OCTOBER 1879

Henry Bidwell, who was born in Bristol on this date, played just once for Rovers, in a friendly game against Aston Villa in April 1897 to mark the official opening of Eastville Stadium. The third of ten children to the chairmaker Charles Bidwell and his wife Harriet, Henry Bidwell married Mary Jane Taylor in Bristol in 1902 and continued to live in the city. In opening the new stadium, Rovers called on the league and FA Cup winners Villa, who brought an experienced side to Bristol and trounced Bidwell's side by five goals to nil.

SATURDAY 29TH OCTOBER 1932

Before a crowd of 7,000, Rovers recorded a 3-0 win away to Clapton Orient. Viv Gibbins, an England international who scored all three goals, was an amateur player and the only amateur to complete a Football League season as Rovers' top scorer. Indeed, he is one of only three players to have achieved this feat in the Football League since 1919. Gibbins was top scorer for West Ham United in 1930-31 with 18 goals, and for Rovers, in 1932-33, with 14 goals. Claude Mortimore equalled this achievement in 1949-50 with Aldershot, as did George Bromilow with Southport in both 1955-56 and 1956-57.

WEDNESDAY 30TH OCTOBER 1935

Davie Walker, who scored 28 goals in 78 Southern League matches in two spells with Rovers, died in Walsall at the age of 51. Born in Oakdene, near Walsall, in 1884, the fifth of nine children to a coalpit puddler and engineer, Walker joined Rovers initially in May 1905, having played for Wolves in two First Division games. After two seasons, he was off to West Bromwich Albion and later Leicester Fosse, but he rejoined Rovers in June 1911. By 1912, the lure of the Midlands proved too strong again and Walker joined Willenhall Swifts and later Walsall.

SATURDAY 30TH OCTOBER 1982

An Eastville crowd of 7,270, who had seen four home goals in each of the last three matches, was treated to a comfortable 3-0 victory over Reading. David Williams scored twice and Graham Withey once in this Third Division fixture. At this stage in the season, the side recorded 20 goals in five consecutive home league matches, though the goals later dried up.

SATURDAY 31ST OCTOBER 1908

Walter Raynor of Norwich City was sent off at Eastville for head-butting Rovers' Billy Peplow, who also received his marching orders for retaliating. Rovers won this Southern League match 2-0 before a 10,000 crowd. Peplow, born in Derby in 1885 and a recent signing from Birmingham, was to play for Rovers in 216 Southern League matches and score 42 goals. Peplow had opened the scoring and John Roberts added the second goal.

FRIDAY 31st OCTOBER 1958

Having played in 486 league games for Rovers, full-back Harry Bamford was an intrinsic part of the club's fabric. The 38-year-old had been coaching schoolboys at Clifton College when his motorcycle was involved in a collision with a car. For three days his life hung in the balance before he died of his injuries on the last day of the month. At a memorial service in St. Mary Redcliffe, manager Bert Tann said that "a part of Bristol Rovers died with him". Certainly, his untimely death brought to an end a golden era in the club's history that had seen promotion and two FA Cup quarter-final appearances.

SATURDAY 31st OCTOBER 1987

A crowd of 4,487 at Griffin Park saw Rovers recover a half-time deficit to draw 1-1 with Brentford in a Third Division fixture. Unchanged following a 4-0 drubbing of Doncaster Rovers seven days earlier, Rovers were indebted to Gary Penrice's tenth league goal of the season, after Paul Williams, on loan from Charlton Athletic, had given the home side the lead before the interval.

BRISTOL ROVERS
On This Day

NOVEMBER

SATURDAY 1ST NOVEMBER 1952

In two separate matches in November 1952, Rovers scored four goals in 18 minutes. In front of a crowd of 26,858 at home to Reading, John McIlvenny's 15th-minute goal was followed by further strikes from Geoff Bradford two minutes later and Vic Lambden after 25 minutes. Ray Warren's penalty, his final goal for the club, preceded a goalless second half. Two home games later, Rovers repeated the feat against Brighton & Hove Albion with four quick goals in a match that was won comfortably by seven goals to nil.

SATURDAY 2ND NOVEMBER 1946

Rovers have rarely played in red. One such game was a 3-0 defeat at Watford in April 1935, when Rovers wore an all-red kit. For the 4-0 defeat in front of a 35,000 crowd at Cardiff City in 1946, Rovers wore red and white quarters to avoid a colour clash. Already a goal down to Stanley Richards' third-minute strike, Rovers lost goalkeeper Jack Weare through injury after only seven minutes and the ten men lost heavily. Richards scored a second goal with Billy Rees and Bryn Allen adding one apiece.

SATURDAY 3RD NOVEMBER 2001

Rovers lost 2-0 at Aggborough against Kidderminster Harriers in a basement division game that attracted a crowd of 3,588. Scott Jones, Martin Cameron, Simon Bryant and Ronnie Maugé returned to the side, after a run of seven games without a win, but the Kidderminster match was the first of five in succession without a league goal. Rovers' first-ever season in the bottom tier of the Football League proved much harder than initially believed and only the dismal form of bottom club Halifax Town saved Rovers the worry of an end-of-season scrap to ensure the retention of league status.

SATURDAY 4TH NOVEMBER 1911

The highest attendance at any Southern League game at Eastville was the 16,000 who came to see the game against Queens Park Rangers, which was lost 2-0. Rovers were also defeated in the return fixture – Jim Brogan and Jim Peplow both scoring in a 4-2 defeat – as QPR secured the divisional championship, pipping Plymouth Argyle by a single point; Rovers finished fourth from bottom.

SATURDAY 4TH NOVEMBER 1950

Taunted by Plymouth Argyle supporters singing Goodnight Irene when a goal up through Maurice Tadman, the brother of a pre-war Rovers forward, Rovers' home crowd amongst the 29,654 attendance regained the initiative after half-time. Three Rovers goals in eight second-half minutes from George Petherbridge, Geoff Bradford and Vic Lambden led to renditions of Goodnight Argyle and this Huddie Ledbetter song was adopted for the first time by the Eastville crowd. Into the 21st-century the lyrics remain very popular with the Gas faithful and an iconic song amongst Bristol Rovers supporters.

MONDAY 4TH NOVEMBER 1968

Scottish-born winger Ken Ronaldson scored one of Rovers' goals in a 4-2 home win against Barrow to become the first Rovers substitute to get his name on the score-sheet in a league fixture. Bobby Jones scored two (one penalty) and Harold Jarman one for Rovers, with Jim Mulvaney and Roy McCarthy scoring for Barrow before a crowd of 4,937. Substitutes had only been permitted in league matches since the start of the 1965-66 season. Graham Withey in 1982, Mark Walters in 2001 and Andy Rammell in 2003 have all scored twice in a league game for Rovers after coming on as substitute.

SATURDAY 5TH NOVEMBER 1898

A sixth consecutive unbeaten Birmingham and District League fixture was secured with a comfortable 6-0 victory away to Worcester Rovers. Jack Jones, a prolific goalscorer at all levels of football, completed a hat-trick, Dave Smellie scored twice and George Brown added the sixth. Rovers scored 132 goals that season in just 34 matches and were unsurprisingly awarded a place in the Southern League for 1899-1900.

SATURDAY 5TH NOVEMBER 1927

Rovers' reserve side led 1-0 at half-time at home to Exeter City reserves, thanks to a goal from Roy Davies direct from a corner. From then on, though, things fell apart. Bill Culley and Albert Rotherham both scored own goals, the hapless Culley also missed a penalty and Rovers second XI lost 5-1. The first team fared no better that day, Fred Dent scoring four times for Exeter City who won 4-1 at St James' Park.

THURSDAY 5TH NOVEMBER 1992

Rovers broke their record for the highest transfer fee paid in signing central defender Andy Tillson from Queens Park Rangers for a fee of £370,000. This club record transfer was an unusual affair, as Tillson was signed by the club's directors on a tip-off from former Rovers manager Gerry Francis. Tillson, whose career had started at Grimsby Town, was born in Huntingdon in the World Cup summer of 1966 and played in 250 (plus three as substitute) league matches for Rovers, scoring eleven goals, before leaving the club in 2000.

SUNDAY 6TH NOVEMBER 1960

Gary Clarke, who played in six (plus five as substitute) league games for Rovers between 1978 and 1980 as a winger, was born in Boston, Lincolnshire. Brought up in Bristol, Clarke was on Bristol City's books with his twin brother Craig and joined Rovers as an apprentice in July 1977. He scored against his former club in an Anglo-Scottish Cup-tie, but never repeated the feat in the league and joined Bath City in 1980.

FRIDAY 7TH NOVEMBER 1735

The discovery of three men and a boy, who had all been missing underground for almost eleven days, provoked great relief in the tight-knit coal mining community around Rovers' heartland. The four miners had been 39 fathoms below the surface in a mine at Two Mile Hill and found themselves on the edge of a precipice in darkness. Full of fear, they apparently found a hollow and waited, one having a knife with which to cut stale bread. Then they lost the knife. When they were found, after ten days and 19 hours, the oldest, a 60-year-old, was delirious, but all four were able to walk home.

SATURDAY 7TH NOVEMBER 1931

On only five occasions, Rovers have scored five goals before half-time in a league fixture. One such game was the home fixture with Gillingham, in which Rovers raced to a 5-0 half-time lead, with Eric Oakton, Frank Townrow (2), Tommy Cook and Bert Young scoring. Gillingham recovered after the break, the England cricketer Les Ames scoring their second goal in a 5-2 defeat.

WEDNESDAY 8TH NOVEMBER 1972

Marcus Stewart, who scored for Rovers at Wembley in the unsuccessful play-off final against Huddersfield Town in 1995, was born in Bristol. Stewart scored goals from an early age and had eleven England schoolboy caps to his name. Overall, he played in 137 (plus 34 as substitute) league matches for Rovers, scoring 57 goals, before joining Huddersfield in July 1997. He went on to play for Ipswich Town, Sunderland, Bristol City, Preston, Yeovil Town and Exeter City.

SUNDAY 9TH NOVEMBER 1800

The floods were so bad in the Eastville area that part of Stapleton Bridge was carried away by the water. There have been floods on many occasions down the years in these parts, especially the devastating floods of 1607, 1703, 1720, 1738, 1800, 1882, 1889 and several years in the 20th century. Rising water is a recurrent theme in the Rovers story, and this is reflected in the evocative and oft-recalled lyrics of the supporters' favourite song, Goodnight Irene.

SATURDAY 10TH NOVEMBER 1934

Leading 3-0 after 30 minutes and 5-2 with only eight minutes to go, Rovers had to settle for a point in the home game against Exeter City. Jimmy Smith, who had claimed a British seasonal record with an astonishing 72 goals with Ayr United in 1927-28, scored three times for Rovers, whilst George Tadman and Jack Allen scored once each, before an Eastville crowd of 9,500. The future Rovers wing-half Harold Webb scored the Grecians' first goal from the penalty spot, before Henry Poulter and Frank Wrightson scored two apiece.

SATURDAY 11TH NOVEMBER 1995

Rovers suffered an FA Cup nightmare in front of a crowd of 3,001 at Hitchin Town. As if being drawn away to Hitchin was not enough to strike anticipatory fear into the mind of any Rovers supporter, the ICIS Premier Division side took the lead through a Steve Conroy header after only 47 seconds and went further ahead when Lee Burns chipped an outstanding second in the ninth minute. Rovers were able to pull one goal back, through Lee Archer, but Hitchin Town held on for a thoroughly deserved 2-1 victory.

SATURDAY 12TH NOVEMBER 1904

Rovers' reserve side defeated HMS Antelope 18-2 at Eastville, having stormed into an unassailable half-time lead of 11-2. Fred Latham and Walter Gerrish scored six goals each, Jimmy Shervey added three and there were two goals for Walter Pickett and one for the former Bristol City wing-half Bill Hales. Gerrish, who later won a league championship medal with Aston Villa, was killed during World War I.

SATURDAY 13TH NOVEMBER 1982

In a bizarre numerical oddity, five Rovers players in consecutively numbered shirts scored in a Third Division victory over promotion favourites Portsmouth at Eastville. Rovers' scorers in a 5-1 win were: Tim Parkin (5), Aidan McCaffrey (6), Ian Holloway (7), David Williams (8) and Archie Stephens (9). Before a crowd of 9,389, all Pompey had to show from the game was a very late consolation goal from Billy Rafferty.

THURSDAY 14TH NOVEMBER 1946

Kenny Stephens, a winger who had played for West Bromwich Albion and Walsall before signing for Rovers, was born in Bristol. A Rovers player from October 1970, Stephens scored on his debut at Barnsley and contributed eleven goals in 215 (plus ten as substitute) league matches in his time with Rovers before signing for Hereford United in October 1977. He was later chairman of Hanham Athletic for many years.

SATURDAY 15TH NOVEMBER 1958

After a quiet start, the 7-3 Second Division victory over Grimsby Town at Eastville exploded into life just before half-time. Dai Ward, after 28 minutes, and Peter Hooper, eleven minutes later, gave Rovers a 2-0 lead, only for Tommy Briggs, whose seven goals for Blackburn Rovers had sunk the Eastville side in February 1955, to pull one back a minute before half-time. Ward extended Rovers' lead and Mike Cullen replied for Grimsby before two Hooper goals in four minutes completed his hat-trick and left Rovers 5-2 ahead, before Ron Rafferty pulled a goal back 14 minutes from time. Geoff Bradford, however, scored twice in five minutes, three Rovers players registered doubles – as against Middlesbrough in November 1955 – and Rovers had avenged the 7-0 drubbing of eleven months earlier.

SUNDAY 16TH NOVEMBER 1930

It was seen as a matter of surprise in the press that Rovers did not defeat Holland more easily, given the tourists' natural skill and fitness compared with perceived Dutch tactical naivety. A narrow 3-2 victory in Amsterdam was achieved through two Ronnie Dix goals and one from Arthur Attwood, Gerrit Hulsman scoring twice for the Dutch, though one looked suspiciously offside. The star turn was the Dutch outside-right Adje Gerritse, who gave Rovers' long-suffering left-back John Richardson a torrid afternoon. Rovers played this game on a Sunday, having completed a rough North Sea crossing after a Saturday league fixture.

SATURDAY 16TH NOVEMBER 1946

Six goals were conceded at Meadow Lane, where a crowd of 14,390 saw Notts County brush Rovers aside 6-0. Rovers were already 3-0 down inside 26 minutes, long before the future England international Jackie Sewell scored two goals in a minute, just past the hour mark, both from long, sweeping moves by the home side. The veteran Harry Smith became Rovers' oldest-ever Football League debutant, five weeks past his 38th birthday; he was to play three times for the club before taking on a senior coaching role.

SATURDAY 17TH NOVEMBER 1900

Rovers were expected to defeat Weymouth in the FA Cup but a poor attendance reflects the fact that few would have predicted the glut of goals. Hill Griffiths put Rovers ahead with a tap-in after only three minutes, while Jack Jones, with two long-range shots, and Billy Williams had scored twice each before the visitors' centre-forward Murphy pulled a goal back on the stroke of half-time. Rovers then scored ten second-half goals to record a 15-1 victory, the club's record score in any competitive first-team match. Billy Clarke scored a second-half hat-trick, his second goal being a spectacular long distance strike, while Williams ended up with three goals and Jones, six. Hill Griffiths scored his second of the game, Rovers' 13th and John Paul scored the 15th. This was the only occasion a Rovers player has scored six goals in one game, though Jones almost repeated the feat twelve months later against the same opposition. It was also the only time three Rovers players have scored hat-tricks in the same game.

FRIDAY 17TH NOVEMBER 1989

It was unlikely that a club of the stature of Rovers could have been involved in the first British £1,000,000 transfer of a goalkeeper. However, Nigel Martyn had proved he was an outstanding custodian and had compiled a tally of 101 league appearances for Rovers since being signed from the Cornish side St. Blazey in August 1987. After his million-pound transfer to Crystal Palace he played for his new side between the sticks in the 1990 FA Cup Final, before going on to win 23 full caps for England.

SATURDAY 17TH NOVEMBER 2007

The earliest goal in a league game involving Rovers that a substitute has scored is seven minutes. Millwall's Ali Fuseini's entry to replace Alan Dunne had been timed as 4 minutes 40 seconds and he gave his side the lead after 7 minutes 49 seconds. Rovers recovered to win 2-1 in this League One game at the Memorial Stadium before 6,991 fans. Rickie Lambert, from a penalty, and Lewis Haldane scored for Rovers.

SATURDAY 18TH NOVEMBER 1972

Just five weeks after winning at Old Trafford in the League Cup, Rovers suffered the ignominy of losing an FA Cup tie 1-0 away to Isthmian League side Hayes. The Middlesex side, cheered on by a crowd of 6,000, fully deserved their win which came courtesy of Bobby Hatt's goal nine minutes after half-time. Hayes' star turn that day was 20-year-old Robin Friday, who was on the verge of an entertaining and maverick career in football.

SATURDAY 18TH NOVEMBER 1978

The second and most recent occasion that Rovers have drawn a league game 5-5 came when Charlton Athletic, undefeated away from home, visited Eastville for a Second Division fixture. Rovers had won all seven home league games to that point, but trailed early to Dick Tydeman's goal. Although Paul Randall scored twice to put Rovers ahead, Charlton were to lead 3-2 at half-time and 5-3 after 63 minutes. All ten goals came in a frenetic 53-minute spell, with Randall scoring three and David Williams two for Rovers, Martyn Robinson (2) and Mick Flanagan (2) adding to Tydeman's opener for Charlton.

SATURDAY 19TH NOVEMBER 1968

On the day Rovers ran up a 5-1 win at home to Gillingham, their future midfielder Justin Channing was born in Reading. A defensive midfielder, he played for Queens Park Rangers before signing for Rovers, initially on loan in October 1992, and later for £250,000. Channing's ten league goals in 121 (plus nine as substitute) appearances for Rovers included a hat-trick as Barnet were defeated 5-2 at Twerton Park. He joined Leyton Orient in 1996.

SATURDAY 20TH NOVEMBER 1999

So unexpected was David Pritchard's only league goal in 157 (plus six as substitute) league appearances for Rovers – which came in a 1-0 win at Chesterfield watched by a crowd of 2,875 – that one Gas supporter had to honour a bet and walk home from the ground. Nineteen-year-old Ben Davies found five friends to accompany him on this 154-mile walk and they raised a total of £3,255.70 for Macmillan Cancer Research and the Supporters' Club 'Raise the Roof' Fund.

SATURDAY 21ST NOVEMBER 1925

A dull, goalless draw at Millwall, where Rovers played in front of a crowd of 12,000, was livened by the fact that the Lions' half-back Syd Gore contrived to miss two penalties during the match. Three weeks later, when Millwall were again awarded two penalties Alf Amos took and scored both, as his side led 6-0 by half-time at home to Luton Town. Prior to Rovers' game at Millwall, there was a one-minute silence to the memory of Alexandra, the Queen Mother and widow of King Edward VII, who had died the previous day.

TUESDAY 21ST NOVEMBER 1950

There was water seven feet deep on the Eastville pitch after some of the heaviest rainstorms for many years. Rovers' history is intertwined with stories of water and flooding and Eastville suffered badly until the Northern Stormwater Interceptor was finally opened in 1968. Much of the River Frome is now intercepted at Eastville and taken underground to join the Avon at the Portway below Clifton Downs. Prior to this, stories of flooding were commonplace, so much so that the evocative lyrics of Goodnight Irene reflect this situation.

MONDAY 22ND NOVEMBER 1982

Simon Bryant, who was Rovers' youngest ever captain as well as the third youngest player ever to appear for the side in the league, was born in Bristol. A brother of a Bristol City and Gillingham defender, Bryant was seen as Rovers' most exciting prospect in some time. He played in midfield in 58 (plus 17 as substitute) appearances scoring twice, from his debut in August 1999 to his July 2004 move to Forest Green Rovers.

FRIDAY 23RD NOVEMBER 1956

Bob Newton, an experienced striker who played in seven (plus one as substitute) league games for Rovers without scoring at the tail end of the 1986-87 season, was born in Chesterfield. A goalscorer in the 1974 FA Youth Cup final, Newton had played for Huddersfield Town, Hartlepool United, Port Vale, Stockport County and Chesterfield before ending his career with Rovers. Later a player in America and Hong Kong, Newton became a long-distance lorry driver.

SATURDAY 24TH NOVEMBER 2007

Rovers' single-goal defeat at Swindon Town was notable for the sending-off of four players, two from each side. Swindon's Jerel Ifil was shown a red card along with Rovers pair Steve Elliott and substitute Richard Walker. They were later joined by Swindon substitute Sofiane Zaaboub, just two minutes after he had entered the field of play. A crowd of 9,342 was present at The County Ground. The game was decided by a Christian Roberts penalty for Swindon midway through the second half.

SATURDAY 25TH NOVEMBER 1893

Rovers' fourth win of the season in the Bristol and District League was an ultimately comfortable 4-2 victory over Trowbridge Town in front of a crowd of 600 in their first game on the club's new ground at Rudgway. Bob Horsey scored twice, including Rovers' first goal at this new venue, and Bill Rogers and Bill Taylor claimed a goal apiece. Horsey was to be Rovers' top scorer with eight goals in 18 matches as Rovers finished ninth in the table and appears to have scored 36 goals in 126 appearances for Rovers in the ill-documented early years of the club.

SATURDAY 26TH NOVEMBER 1921

For the first time since elevation to the Football League, Rovers found their match abandoned, as fog descended on Elm Park. The game was stopped just seven minutes into the second half, with Rovers leading 3-1 through two goals from Sid Leigh and one from Joe Walter. When the game was finally played, Reading ran out 4-0 winners before a crowd of 6,000 at Elm Park, their centre-forward Sam Jennings scoring a hat-trick.

SATURDAY 27TH NOVEMBER 1937

Having drawn with the same opposition in the league weeks earlier, Rovers crashed to a humiliating 8-1 defeat at home to Queens Park Rangers to equal their worst ever score in the FA Cup. An Eastville crowd of 8,869, which produced gate receipts of £520, was stunned as Rangers scored five times in 17 first-half minutes, with Alf Fitzgerald scoring a first-half hat-trick, Tom Cheetham also scoring three and Wilf Bott adding two more. Bill Pendergast scored a consolation goal after 55 minutes. Rovers' manager Percy Smith was sacked in the aftermath of this defeat.

SATURDAY 27TH NOVEMBER 1999

In beating Luton Town 3-0 at the Memorial Stadium, Rovers outlined their potential promotion credentials. A crowd of 7,805 saw Andy Thomson and Mark Walters before half-time, as well as Jamie Cureton after 48 minutes, give the Gas a comfortable home win. This third in a run of six straight victories lifted Rovers to fourth in the table.

SUNDAY 28TH NOVEMBER 1948

Mick Channon, the vastly experienced striker who played in four (plus five more as substitute) league matches with Rovers in the autumn of 1982, was born in the Wiltshire village of Orcheston. In over 500 league matches with Southampton, Channon had scored a club record 185 goals for the Saints. He also played for Manchester City, Newcastle United, Norwich City and Portsmouth, winning 46 England caps in addition to an FA Cup winner's medal with Southampton in 1976 and a League Cup winner's medal nine years later with Norwich City. Mick Channon is now a well-respected racehorse owner based in Berkshire, where he runs a successful stable.

SATURDAY 29TH NOVEMBER 1952

After George Petherbridge's 18th-minute opener, Rovers scored six second-half goals to defeat Brighton & Hove Albion 7-0 in a Third Division (South) fixture, a tally for one half equalled only in the game at Reading in January 1999. Bill Roost scored twice, after 48 and 70 minutes, either side of the predictable goals from Vic Lambden on 53 minutes and Geoff Bradford seven minutes later. Petherbridge claimed his second goal before the luckless Reg Fox put through his own goal two minutes from time. Rovers had scored four goals in 18 minutes and six in one glorious 40-minute spell.

MONDAY 29TH NOVEMBER 1965

It was easy to travel early in the 20th-century to Eastville Stadium. Stapleton Road railway station, a short walk from the ground, had been opened to passenger and freight transport on September 8th 1863 and served the surrounding area for over one hundred years. Now it was to shut to goods traffic, leaving only a relatively sporadic service for football fans on foot.

SATURDAY 30TH NOVEMBER 1946

The FA Cup brought Rovers no joy as, for the first time since elevation to the Football League in 1920 the club was knocked out by a non-league side. Rovers visited Penydarren Park, where a crowd of 14,000 saw Merthyr Town defeat their deflated opponents 3-1. Captain Bill Hullett scored twice for the home side, whose other goalscorer, George Crisp, had played for Rovers during the 1935-36 season. Rovers had led at the interval through Vic Lambden's 20th-minute goal.

SATURDAY 30TH NOVEMBER 1996

A crowd of 4,496 witnessed an extraordinary 4-3 success at home to Bury. Peter Beadle scored a nine-minute hat-trick shortly before half-time (30, 38, 39 minutes), only for Bury to pull back two goals in first-half injury time. Billy Clark's only goal of the season, just seconds after the interval, was the sixth goal inside 16 minutes. Bury were Second Division champions this season, this defeat being the only league game in which the Shakers conceded four goals. Bury's scorers were David Pugh, David Johnson and Mark Carter (penalty).

BRISTOL ROVERS
On This Day

DECEMBER

SATURDAY 1st DECEMBER 1883

Rovers' first ever game was played at Wotton-under-Edge with Rovers, then known as The Black Arabs, being heavily defeated 6-0. No match report or team line-ups have survived and local contemporary press reports were scant. However, two line-ups do exist for games later in the 1883-84 season and these indicate that it is likely that Rovers would have included Harry Horsey, Bill Braund, Richard Conyers, Fred Hall and Bill Davies in their side and would possibly have been captained by left-half Henry Martin. This Henry Martin was a 20-year-old Bristolian, the eldest of nine children to George Martin, a shipwright, and his wife Emily.

SATURDAY 1st DECEMBER 1973

Rovers' record league win, an 8-2 victory at Brighton which was broadcast on national television, was a demoralising blow to Albion's young manager, Brian Clough. In front of a crowd of 10,762, Bruce Bannister put Rovers ahead after four minutes, Gordon Fearnley made it 2-0 eight minutes later and, though the Welsh international Peter O'Sullivan pulled a goal back, Rovers were 5-1 ahead by the break. Bannister had already completed what was to be the only hat-trick of his Rovers career. After half-time, Alan Warboys took over, adding three more to his first-half goal to become only the second Rovers player to score four goals in an away league game. He could have had more, too, had he not been forced to leave the field at one stage to have stitches inserted in a cut above his eye. Ronnie Howell's 87th minute consolation goal could not deprive Rovers of a record league win, on the day the reserves won 6-1 against their Bristol City counterparts. No other Division Three fixture has ever finished in an 8-2 win for the away side.

MONDAY 2nd DECEMBER 1940

The Purdown gun-site overlooking Rovers' Eastville stadium was bombed overnight and there were two fatalities, Gunner Frederick Oxenham and Volunteer David Acraman Greenslade. The latter was a 19-year-old from Bradford-upon-Avon, who was serving with the 11th Gloucestershire Battalion. His death formed the first part of a double family tragedy, as his father, Arthur Acraman Greenslade, was killed two months later in active service. Both are buried at Canford Cemetery in Bristol.

TUESDAY 2ND DECEMBER 1997

Nothing could have prepared Rovers for the five red cards issued on a frosty evening in Wigan in December by referee Kevin Lynch. Ian Kilford and David Lowe, with two goals, scored in Wigan Athletic's 3-0 win in front of a crowd of 2,738 at Springfield Park. David Pritchard received a second yellow card only seconds before half-time and was promptly joined by Jason Perry, Andy Tillson and Wigan's Graeme Jones for alleged pushing while the resultant free kick was about to be taken. These decisions were viewed by many as harsh, as was Josh Low's second-half dismissal for a second booking, in a game generally considered fair and clean. Nonetheless, seven-man Rovers, only the second league club to suffer this fate, after Hereford United in November 1992, made the headlines for all the wrong reasons.

SATURDAY 3RD DECEMBER 1927

A flurry of six goals in a spell of just 15 minutes as half-time approached marked Rovers' 4-3 defeat in an enthralling game to treat a 6,000 crowd at Bournemouth. The home side took the lead four times in this match, with Ron Eyre scoring twice, though Rovers' players claimed the second had not crossed the line; Theophilus Pike added the second-half winner. Rovers' three equalisers had come courtesy of 37-year-old Bill Culley (2) and a strike from Jack Evans that makes him Rovers' all-time oldest league goalscorer – he was just a few weeks short of his 39th birthday.

MONDAY 4TH DECEMBER 1933

Ron Nicholls, a tall and reliable goalkeeper who also enjoyed a long career in county cricket, was born in Sharpness, Gloucestershire. Nicholls joined Rovers in November 1954 and played in 71 league matches, before continuing his career with Cardiff City and Bristol City. At this time, both Nicholls and Barrie Meyer, later a celebrated Test umpire, were in Rovers' side though their association with the club came to an eventual end because of the conflict of interests whenever pre-season training clashed with county cricket commitments. An outstanding cricketer, Nicholls played in 534 cricket matches for Gloucestershire, and is their fourth highest scorer with over 23,000 runs to his name. Nicholls died in Cheltenham in July 1994 at the age of 60.

WEDNESDAY 5TH DECEMBER 1973

Paul Tovey, who enjoyed a brief career in Rovers' midfield in the 1990s, was born in Wokingham. One of several players tried out during a changeable time in the club's fortunes, Tovey played in eight (plus one as substitute) league matches for Rovers before signing for Bath City in July 1996. Following 17 (plus four as substitute) appearances for the Twerton Park club, he later played for Yate Town, Clevedon Town and Paulton Rovers.

TUESDAY 6TH DECEMBER 1949

The death of Huddie 'Lead Belly' Ledbetter in New York at the age of 60 preceded Rovers' adoption as a club song of his most famous rendition, Goodnight Irene, an old mixed-race song emanating from 1880s Cincinnati, Ohio. Lead Belly, born on a plantation near Mooringsport in Louisiana on January 20th 1888, had spent time in jail for homicide and claimed to have learned Goodnight Irene in 1918 from his uncle Terrell Ledbetter, who had encouraged his early musical interest. "(Lead Belly's) arms were like big stove pipes, his face was powerful and he picked the twelve-string guitar," said the commentator Woody Guthrie. Rovers adopted this anthem as the club's own in 1950 and the legend grew with it, so that it is now sung with gusto at every game.

TUESDAY 6TH DECEMBER 1983

Rovers' centenary celebrations involved a prestigious match against Newcastle United, partly as it was viewed that one of Rovers' most glorious hours had been the 1951 FA Cup quarter-final tie against the Magpies. Before a crowd of 4,107, Rovers defeated Newcastle 5-4 at Eastville, with the prolific striker Paul Randall scoring a hat-trick.

SATURDAY 7TH DECEMBER 1929

By half-time in this Third Division (South) match against Bournemouth, the Eastville pitch had turned into a quagmire and the referee had little option but to abandon the game, the first such occasion for Rovers in a home Football League match. By this stage Rovers were trailing 1-0, Bournemouth's goal having been scored by Ron Eyre, who nonetheless scored 15 times in his 15 completed league games against Rovers, more than any other opponent has ever managed.

SATURDAY 7TH DECEMBER 1935

When Rovers travelled to Aldershot for a Third Division (South) match, an interesting event took place in a Hampshire court. The Aldershot chairman was also a local magistrate and the defendant before him is alleged to have pleaded: "Please, Sir, can I have bail so that I can go and see the Rovers beat Aldershot?" The request was turned down and Rovers, although Vince Harwood scored before a crowd of 2,000, lost 6-1. At that time it was the home side's largest league victory, centre-forward Bert Lutterloch completing a hat-trick. This was not Rovers' heaviest defeat of the season, though, for the Easter Monday trip to Luton Town's Kenilworth Road resulted in a disastrous 12-0 defeat.

SATURDAY 7TH DECEMBER 1974

The largest number of goals scored in a Rovers league match after a goalless first-half is seven. Unable to score before half-time, Oldham Athletic and Rovers served up a veritable goal feast for the 9,759 spectators at Boundary Park, which Rovers eventually won 4-3. Ian Robins scored twice for the Latics whilst Maurice Whittle converted a penalty. Gordon Fearnley scored twice, and Alan Warboys and Jeff Coombes got Rovers' other goals.

SATURDAY 8TH DECEMBER 1917

Bill Weston scored nine times as Rovers defeated the Great Western Railway Carriage XI 13-0 in a wartime fixture; Ellis Crompton also scored twice, whilst Edward Skuse and Len Gyles added a goal apiece. There were many very large wins during World War I – the 20-0 victory over the same opposition in February 1919 being the largest – but this was the only occasion one individual player had scored as many times as nine in one particular game.

SATURDAY 8TH DECEMBER 1962

The only footballer to have opposed Rovers in the Football League and played in the NFL for an American Football team was Bobby Howfield, who was in the Watford side defeated 1-0 at Vicarage Road in December 1962 by a Keith Williams goal. Howfield, who also played for Crewe Alexandra, Aldershot and Fulham, spent seven years in gridiron football with Denver Broncos and New York Jets, kicking 76 field goals from 119 attempts.

SATURDAY 8TH DECEMBER 1984

The two professional sides in Bristol met in an FA Cup second-round tie before a crowd of 19,367 at Ashton Gate, where Rovers gained ample revenge for the previous season's result by beating Bristol City 3-1. Gas supporters were stunned as City took an early lead through Bruce Halliday. However, Mark O'Connor scored Rovers' first and Paul Randall added two more before half-time to complete a noteworthy victory.

SATURDAY 9TH DECEMBER 1899

Herbert Chapman was a highly successful manager between the wars, establishing sides at both Arsenal and Huddersfield Town that won three consecutive Football League titles. He was also an inside-forward in his day, appearing in the Sheppey United side that lost a Southern League encounter 3-1 to Rovers. Bill Fisher scored twice for Rovers, and Bobby Brown once, with Alf Harrison scoring for the defeated home side before a crowd of 800 in Kent. This victory secured a 'double', as Rovers had beaten Sheppey 2-1 in the first home game of the season.

SATURDAY 10TH DECEMBER 1988

It was a humiliating afternoon for Rovers in the FA Cup, in which, after a goalless first half, Rovers lost 2-1 to Kettering Town before a crowd of 4,950 at Rockingham Road. All they had to show for their efforts was an Andy Reece consolation goal after 70 minutes. Kettering featured several experienced players, including Lil Fuccillo and Ernie Moss. The former Peterborough United and Brentford striker Robbie Cooke scored both their goals. Nonetheless, it was a demoralising and embarrassing result in front of the BBC *Match of the Day* cameras.

SATURDAY 11TH DECEMBER 1897

Though later equalled in the 1930s at home to QPR, Rovers' highly demoralising 8-1 defeat at The Dell remains the club's heaviest loss in the FA Cup. To be fair, Southampton were Southern League champions and their class showed as Birmingham and District League side Rovers conceded eight goals before a crowd of 8,000, with forwards Jimmy Yates, Bob Buchanan, Watty Keay and Joe Turner scoring two goals each, and inside-forward Jim Cotterell replying for Rovers. The Saints were FA Cup semi-finalists that season.

TUESDAY 11TH DECEMBER 1973

Perhaps the most unusual venue for a football transfer was the evening roadside rendezvous at which Rovers' goalkeeper Dick Sheppard joined Torquay United on loan. Sheppard, born in Bristol in February 1945, had made his name with West Bromwich Albion and his 151 league appearances for Rovers were truncated by a depressed fracture of the skull. With Jim Eadie in goal, Rovers loaned Sheppard to Torquay for two Fourth Division matches. He later played for Weymouth, Portway Bristol and Paulton Rovers and died in Bristol in October 1998, at the age of 53.

SATURDAY 12TH DECEMBER 1936

David Pyle, who played in 139 league games for Rovers without scoring, was born in Trowbridge. A Wiltshire County youth cap, Pyle was a central defender who played for Rovers in Division Two. He made his debut in March 1957 and appeared in the FA Cup quarter-final against Fulham twelve months later. In July 1962 the strong and tough-tackling defender joined Bristol City and played eight times for the Ashton Gate club, before running a succession of pubs in Bristol and back in Wiltshire. He died in February 2002 in Trowbridge, aged 65.

SATURDAY 13TH DECEMBER 1969

A 3-1 defeat at Fulham in Division Three was notable for the fact that the clubs were managed by father and son. Bill Dodgin, an inter-war player who had returned as manager, was in charge of Rovers, whilst his son, Bill Dodgin Junior, was manager of Fulham. Harold Jarman scored Rovers' goal before a crowd of 6,675 at Craven Cottage, whilst John Richardson scored twice, one being a spectacular diving header, and Steve Earle once for Fulham.

SATURDAY 13TH DECEMBER 2003

Hugo Rodrigues is the tallest opponent to face Rovers in league football. The six-feet-eight-inches-tall midfielder played for Yeovil Town in their 1-0 victory at the Memorial Stadium and stands an inch taller than several opponents in recent years. In front of a crowd of 9,812, Nick Crittenden's goal two minutes before half-time earned the visitors a win that was secured even though substitute Jake Edwards had been sent off in the second half.

SATURDAY 14TH DECEMBER 1957

It had been over 30 years since Rovers had lost a league fixture by seven clear goals, but Rovers' all-time heaviest home league defeat was 7-0 at the hands of Grimsby Town. It could have been worse, too, for Ron Rafferty, who had already scored from one penalty, struck a late spot kick over the bar. Three goals ahead at half-time, the Mariners scored through Ron Stockin (2), Gerry Priestley, Johnny Scott (2), Ron Rafferty and Jimmy Fell. During one 18-minute spell, Grimsby scored four goals and missed a penalty.

SATURDAY 14TH DECEMBER 1963

The 50th Bristol derby in the Football League ended in a resounding win for Rovers, a rare glimmer of hope in a depressing season that culminated in relegation to Division Three. An Eastville crowd of 19,451 saw Rovers win 4-0, having scored three times in the opening eleven minutes. Long-range shots from Doug Hillard, after four minutes, and Harold Jarman preceded Alfie Biggs' header from an eleventh-minute Jarman free kick. Five minutes from time, Geoff Bradford headed home from Ian Hamilton's cross for Rovers' fourth, the final strike of his club record 242 league goals for Rovers.

TUESDAY 14TH DECEMBER 1993

The red-haired, tough-tackling wing-half John Black died of cancer in Scunthorpe aged 93. Born in Dunipace in May 1900, his career took him to Sunderland, Nelson, Accrington Stanley, Chesterfield and Luton Town before he signed for Rovers in October 1930. Black played in 49 league matches in Rovers' colours, scoring three times. A younger brother of Adam Black of Leicester City, John worked in the steel industry for many years.

SATURDAY 15TH DECEMBER 1928

Arguably the most bizarre own goal conceded by a Rovers player was the winning strike against Northampton Town in a match played in heavy fog. Having led at half-time through a Jack Phillips goal, Rovers lost 2-1 after goalkeeper Jesse Whatley, and probably the 6,000 crowd, had completely failed to see Jack Cosgrove's harmless back pass. As he looked into the gloom, the ball apparently trickled into the net – just away from him – to give the visitors victory.

SATURDAY 15TH DECEMBER 2001

There have been seven occasions when Rovers have seen their league match abandoned, but only one was stopped before half-time. This was the game against Hartlepool United at the Memorial Stadium, which lasted all of twelve minutes before succumbing to the frost-bound pitch. When the match was replayed, Adam Boyd scored the only goal of the game for the visitors.

SATURDAY 16TH DECEMBER 1893

Arriving with only ten men, Rovers borrowed a player from Wolverton FC for the game against Swindon Athletic. Though Rovers led at the interval through Arthur Williams' only goal for the club, subsequent goals from Robbie Reynolds and Jimmy Hayward earned Athletic a 2-1 victory. The borrowed player was Tom Haycock, a 21-year-old railway carriage wood turner from Buckinghamshire who happened to be at the game that day.

SATURDAY 17TH DECEMBER 1910

In losing 3-2 at Northampton Town in the Southern League, in front of a crowd of 3,000, Rovers conceded a goal scored by a goalkeeper. Ben Hurley and Harry Phillips were Rovers' scorers, with Fred Whittaker and Fred McDiarmid hitting the net for the Cobblers, before goalkeeper Tommy Thorpe fired home the winner from the penalty spot. Bizarrely, Thorpe was the second goalkeeper to score for Rovers' opposition that season. Brentford's Archie Ling had scored the only goal of the game when the Bees visited Eastville that September. This was Brentford's second goal in their three games that season and both had been penalties converted by their goalkeeper.

SATURDAY 18TH DECEMBER 1920

Having not scored in the opening half an hour, six second-half goals eased Rovers to a very comfortable FA Cup victory over Midland Counties League side Worksop Town at Eastville. Before a crowd of 14,000, Rovers strolled to a 9-0 victory, thanks to three goals from Jerry Morgan, two from Sid Leigh and one each from Billy Palmer, Bill Bird, David Kenny and captain Steve Sims. Despite falling short of the 15 goals scored against Weymouth 20 years earlier, Rovers nonetheless progressed to meet Spurs in the next round, a game which was lost 6-2 at White Hart Lane.

WEDNESDAY 18TH DECEMBER 1935

The youngest player to score a hat-trick in a competitive fixture for Rovers was Phil Taylor, who contributed three of Rovers' four goals in an FA Cup second round replay against Oldham Athletic at Eastville, aged 18 years 61 days. Rovers' 4-1 win and a game against Arsenal in the next round came thanks to a fourth goal from Harold 'Happy' Houghton, while the veteran Jack Robson scored for the Latics, before a crowd of 9,550.

SATURDAY 18TH DECEMBER 1948

The oldest side to play against Rovers in the Football League was the Ipswich Town line-up for a Third Division (South) game. Their eleven players had a combined age of over 374 years, giving an average age of 34 years. Their oldest player was 40-year-old outside-left Ossie Parry, whilst centre-forward Tommy Parker, at 24, was the youngest of only three players under thirty. Before a Portman Road crowd of 8,751, Rovers defeated this rather elderly side through a solitary Jimmy Morgan goal.

SATURDAY 18TH DECEMBER 1982

Against Wrexham at Eastville, David Williams put Rovers ahead after half-time before three goals in a purple patch of three minutes – one each from Ian Holloway, Geraint Williams and Brian Williams – gave Rovers a 4-0 victory. Not only do these three goals in three minutes constitute a club fast-scoring record, but this is one of only two occasions when three players with the same surname have scored in a league fixture, the other being when three Keetley brothers scored in Doncaster Rovers' 5-1 win over Durham City in Division Three (North) in April 1927.

SATURDAY 19TH DECEMBER 1925

Aberdare Athletic were frequent opponents of Rovers in league action through the 1920s and one extraordinary game was Rovers' 1-0 victory in South Wales in front of a 4,000 crowd. Five minutes after half-time, with Rovers a goal up through Ernie Whatmore, the Welsh side lost goalkeeper Arthur Brown through injury. Left-back Tom Brophy went in goal, but it was Athletic who attacked. Astonishingly, with John 'Smasher' Smith and David James both missing penalties, Rovers clung on for a narrow victory.

SATURDAY 20TH DECEMBER 2003

With only one win in the last eight league games, Rovers needed a touch of good fortune and it duly arrived at a cold Roots Hall, as Southend United contrived to miss two penalties and present Rovers with three points. First Mark Gower and then Drewe Broughton missed penalties in a league match played before just 3,771 hardy spectators. Dave Savage, after 16 minutes, scored the only goal of the game to earn Rovers a 1-0 victory.

SATURDAY 21ST DECEMBER 1946

There have been precious few occasions when clergymen have appeared in league football. The goalless draw at Eastville with Port Vale featured an opponent, Norman Hallam, who was to become a Methodist minister. Hallam, who was born in Staffordshire in October 1920, also played against Rovers the following season, before retiring in July 1948 to pursue his vocation in the church, having scored four goals in 63 league appearances for the Valiants.

TUESDAY 21ST DECEMBER 1965

The death in Cairo of Mahmoud Mokhtar led to the national stadium being renamed in his honour. Though doubts surround his actual date of birth, it is known that this athlete had represented Egypt at the 1920 Olympic Games in Antwerp before joining Rovers on trial in September 1922. Though unable to break into Rovers' side, Mokhtar was six times Egyptian Player of the Year, won six league championships and seven national cup finals in Egypt and played for his national side in two further Olympics as well as the 1934 World Cup finals in Italy.

SATURDAY 22ND DECEMBER 1928

Rovers lost 2-0 to Coventry City in front of a 14,000 crowd at Highfield Road in a Third Division (South) fixture. The celebrated Ernie Toseland, who was to enjoy a long and illustrious career with Manchester City, scored the opening goal and the second came courtesy of Billy Lake, who was to score four times when the Sky Blues defeated Rovers 5-1 in March 1931. Norman Dinsdale, who played at centre-half, joined Rovers in June 1930 and played in 31 league matches whilst at Eastville, scoring three times.

SATURDAY 22ND DECEMBER 1956

Dai Ward scored the fastest hat-trick recorded by a Rovers player, when he claimed three goals in four minutes of a Second Division game against Doncaster Rovers in front of a crowd of 11,692 at Eastville. The goals came after 77, 78 and 80 minutes, whilst Barrie Meyer scored twice for the second Saturday in succession. The ubiquitous Geoff Bradford added another goal; Rovers won 6-1, with Ron Walker contributing Doncaster's consolation goal.

SATURDAY 23RD DECEMBER 1922

When Rovers faced Brentford in a Division Three (South) game at Griffin Park, both sides fielded famous England cricketers. The Brentford side included Patsy Hendren, who was to appear in 51 Tests for England as well as 138 league games for Brentford, in which he scored 15 goals. Rovers, for their part, fielded an inside-forward by the name of Wally Hammond, who played 20 times for Rovers, scoring twice, 405 times for Gloucestershire and in 85 Test matches for England, top scoring with 336 not out against New Zealand in the summer of 1932.

WEDNESDAY 24TH DECEMBER 1919

Rovers' exciting 3-2 victory at home to Northampton Town in an FA Cup replay was their first game in a run of four matches in four days. Three Southern League games followed, as Rovers lost at Swansea and then drew at home to Swansea and Gillingham. The Northampton game, watched by a Christmas crowd of 14,000, was won through goals from Ted Rawlings, Jimmy Hyam and Ellis Crompton. George Whitworth and Billy Pease replied for the Cobblers.

MONDAY 24TH DECEMBER 1962

Wing-half Jack Howshall, who played in 21 league matches without scoring for Rovers during the 1937-38 season, died in Shelton at the age of 50. Born in Normacott, Staffordshire in July 1912, he had represented Stoke City, Chesterfield and Southport, from whom he joined Rovers in a £350 deal in June 1937. Later with Accrington Stanley and Chesterfield, he found his career cut short by the onset of World War II. Two brothers played professional football, whilst his nephew Gerry Howshall played for West Bromwich Albion and Norwich City.

TUESDAY 25TH DECEMBER 1956

It is unusual to lose 7-2 twice in just over three weeks but, prior to a heavy defeat at Leicester City, Rovers had lost at Gigg Lane by precisely this score. Bury had led 3-1 after 79 minutes, but there were five goals in the final eleven minutes to entertain the crowd of 8,962. Alfie Biggs and George Petherbridge scored for Rovers, whilst Stan Pearson, who claimed three, Tom Neill with two, and Eddie Robertson also with two all scored for Bury; Norman Lockhart's missed penalty saved Rovers from further embarrassment. At 37 years 349 days, Pearson remains the oldest player to score a league hat-trick against Rovers. Twenty-four hours later, in a bizarre juxtaposition of festive results, a Peter Hooper hat-trick eased Rovers to a 6-1 victory over the same opposition.

WEDNESDAY 25TH DECEMBER 1957

The most recent occasion that Rovers have played a league fixture on Christmas Day was the remarkable 6-4 defeat at Swansea. A crowd of 11,340 at Vetch Field saw the bottom club, Swansea, take an early lead through Mel Charles and a Cliff Jones penalty. The Swans went 3-1 up when Ivor Allchurch scored after 38 minutes. By half-time, it was 3-2 to the home side and, though Rovers clawed their way back to 4-4, the Swans eventually ran out deserved 6-4 winners. Jones scored three in total, and Charles two, whilst Peter Sampson, with his first goal in over two years, Dai Ward, Alfie Biggs and Barrie Meyer were the Rovers marksmen.

FRIDAY 26TH DECEMBER 1925

Across almost a century of league football, only seven Rovers players have scored two penalties in a league match. The first was Jonah Wilcox, who thus completed four goals in a fixture. Rovers dominated Bournemouth at Eastville, in front of 12,000 fans and two Albert Burnell goals in the opening five minutes helped the side towards a 4-1 half-time lead. Syd Holcroft scored for Rovers and Wilcox's four strikes, which included two penalties in the final ten minutes, enabled him to equal Sid Leigh's record for goals in a league game. Ron Eyre scored both Bournemouth's goals, his first two of the 15 he registered down the years in league football against Rovers, more than any other opponent.

MONDAY 26TH DECEMBER 1927

Rovers have played in front of a crowd of just 1,000 on only three occasions. There was a goalless draw at Walsall in 1930 and a 2-1 defeat at Torquay in 1933, but the first such occasion was on Boxing Day 1927, when Jim Forbes, Jack Russell and Jack Thom all scored to give Rovers a 3-2 victory over Merthyr Town at Penydarren Park. Welsh international forward Billy Mays scored once in each half for Merthyr.

SUNDAY 26TH DECEMBER 2004

Jamie Forrester's penalty six minutes after half-time earned a point for Rovers, in front of a crowd of 8,414 at the Memorial Stadium, with Rovers reduced to ten men as early as the sixth minute. Robbie Ryan's red card for handball led to the former Gas defender Matt Lockwood opening the scoring from the penalty spot. In the final minute, Rovers brought on 15-year-old Scott Sinclair as a substitute, the club's youngest league player since Ronnie Dix in 1928. The youngster was to play just three minutes' league football for the Pirates before a move to Chelsea kick-started his career.

MONDAY 27TH DECEMBER 1937

Just 48 hours after having beaten the same opposition 5-2 at Eastville, Rovers crashed to Walsall at Fellows Park by the same scoreline, before 8,000 fans. Trailing 4-1 at half-time, Rovers at least rallied through goals from Albert Iles and Bobby Gardiner, whilst Bill Evans (2), Doug Redwood, Ronnie Dodd and right-back Ken Harper scored for Walsall. The home side fielded the talented 17-year-old Bert Williams in goal, a youngster with huge potential, who was destined to play for England after World War II.

SATURDAY 28TH DECEMBER 1935

Arthur Chandler, a legendary name in the East Midlands, remains the only opponent who has scored a league goal against Rovers after his 40th birthday. Born in November 1895, Chandler was just 31 days past 40 when he scored twice for Notts County as they hammered Rovers 6-0 before a crowd of 8,669 at Meadow Lane. Ronnie Green also scored twice, Tom 'Tex' Richards once and Rovers' centre-half Jock McLean deflected the sixth past his own goalkeeper.

SATURDAY 28TH DECEMBER 1957

John Smith, aged 18 years 358 days, remains the youngest opponent to have scored a league hat-trick against Rovers. His three goals enabled West Ham United to defeat Rovers 6-1 in front of an Upton Park crowd of 28,000, with Peter Hooper scoring a consolation goal for Rovers. Vic Keeble also scored twice for the Hammers and John Dick once.

SATURDAY 29TH DECEMBER 1923

With Bournemouth suffering an injury crisis, their left-back Edgar Saxton played in goal for the entire 90 minutes of a Third Division (South) game against Rovers. The away side were 1-0 winners before a 4,000 crowd at Dean Court, with Jimmy Lofthouse's oblique shot after just twelve minutes proving to be the only one Saxton conceded.

SATURDAY 29TH DECEMBER 1928

An extraordinary league fixture at Eastville saw Rovers lose 4-1 to Swindon Town. This was the only time that two Rovers players have ever missed penalties in the same Football League match. In quick succession, Albert Rotherham missed for Rovers, Walter Dickenson of Swindon saw his penalty saved – though he scored from the rebound – and then Jack Phillips' spot kick missed. Rotherham never did score a league goal for Rovers. Phillips did score a consolation goal in this game, watched by a 6,000 crowd, whilst Les Roberts scored Swindon's first goal and Harry Morris added two more.

FRIDAY 30TH DECEMBER 1994

The most celebrated footballer in Rovers' history, Geoff Bradford, died in Bristol at the age of 67. Born in July 1929, Bradford was a free-scoring centre-forward whose 242 goals in 461 league matches for Rovers constitutes a club record that is likely never to be surpassed. A quiet and unassuming man, yet also a talismanic figure, his name appears at each main juncture in Rovers' story over his 15 years with the club. He is also the only man to play for England whilst on Rovers' books, his appearance against Denmark in Copenhagen in October 1955 being marked characteristically by a goal, England's fifth of the game. After retiring from the game, Bradford worked locally and continued to support Rovers, his only league club.

SATURDAY 31st DECEMBER 1938

The last player born in the 19th century to oppose Rovers in league football was Queens Park Rangers' Norman Smith. Having been born in September 1897, he was 41 years 102 days when he played before a crowd of 9,046 in the goalless draw at Eastville on New Year's Eve 1938. A right-back, Smith had played in over 400 league matches for Charlton Athletic, before completing his league career with 68 games and two goals on the books of QPR.

SATURDAY 31st DECEMBER 1966

Goalkeeper Bernard Hall's career was ended after he suffered injuries in an accidental collision with Middlesbrough's John O'Rourke at Eastville. A crowd of 10,645 saw this game, with Doug Hillard and Joe Davis (penalty) scoring for Rovers, while Arthur Horsfield and David Chadwick scored for Boro. Hall, who had played in 163 league matches for Rovers, was unconscious in Frenchay Hospital for 16 days. Though he never resumed his football career, he was able to make a full recovery in terms of his health.